"Cindy N. Ariel gets it like few people do. With a vision that is steeped in both research and experience, she is able to guide us through the trials, confusion, and treasure of loving someone with Asperger's syndrome. She does this with open eyes and an open, compassionate heart. This is the kind of guide I wish for everyone who loves someone who is different."

—Daniel Gottlieb, PhD, psychologist, family therapist, and author of *Letters to Sam* and *The Wisdom of Sam*

"Discovering Asperger's syndrome is a true adventure. But intimate relationships can be complex. Partners most often must learn to reflect, adapt, and compromise for the relationship to succeed. Accepting each partner's differences and reaching mutual understanding can be a long journey. In her book, Ariel truly captures the essence and uniqueness of an Asperger's-neurotypical relationship. With her explanations, examples, and exercises, she guides couples toward better communication, quality time, and intimacy. This book will inspire couples to attain a better relationship."

—Isabelle Hénault, MA, PhD, sexologist, psychologist, and author of *Asperger's Syndrome and Sexuality*

"*Loving Someone with Asperger's Syndrome* is a practical and helpful must-have guide for couples as well as therapists! This easy-to-read book includes lots of AS-friendly exercises based on the learning style of individuals with AS. These tools provide concrete activities that can assist couples in working through issues that commonly occur when one partner has Asperger's."

—Diane Adreon, PhD, associate director of the University of Miami Center for Autism and coauthor of *Asperger Syndrome and Adolescence*

"An informative and practical book that couples will enjoy reading to achieve greater mutual understanding and acquire strategies to enhance their relationship. This book will encourage realistic hope for the future and help partners rediscover and reinforce the deep love that can be felt for someone with Asperger's syndrome.

—Tony Attwood, PhD, author of *The Complete Guide to Asperger's Syndrome*

"Kudos to Cindy N. Ariel! While her new book, *Loving Someone with Asperger's Syndrome*, will be widely used by partners, its potential for use by professionals who are therapists and counselors is remarkable. The exercises help each of the two parties conceptualize what the other is thinking in a blameless, constructive manner so as to support change and adaptation. I fully plan to use this book in my university teaching programs for upcoming social workers."

—Dena L. Gassner, LMSW, owner/director of the Center for Understanding in Nashville, TN, and contributing author to *Scholars with Autism*

loving
someone
with
asperger's
syndrome

Understanding & Connecting
with Your Partner

CINDY N. ARIEL, PhD

New Harbinger Publications, Inc.

Publisher's Note

Distributed in Canada by Raincoast Books

Copyright © 2012 by Cindy N. Ariel
New Harbinger Publications, Inc.
5674 Shattuck Avenue
Oakland, CA 94609
www.newharbinger.com

Cover design by Amy Shoup; Text design by Tracy Marie Carlson; Acquired by Melissa Kirk; Edited by Nelda Street

Printed in the United States of America

Library of Congress Cataloging-in-Publication Data

Ariel, Cindy N.
  Loving someone with Asperger's syndrome : understanding and connecting with your partner / Cindy N. Ariel ; foreword by Stephen Shore.
      p. cm.
  Includes bibliographical references.
  ISBN 978-1-60882-077-1 (pbk.) -- ISBN 978-1-60882-078-8 (pdf e-book) -- ISBN 978-1-60882-079-5 (epub)
  1. Asperger's syndrome--Patients--Family relationships. 2. Spouses. I. Title.
  RC553.A88A4878 2012
  616.85'8832--dc23

                              2011039767

18   17   16

10   9   8   7   6   5.   4

To my partner, Robert, and to the gifts of our relationship:

Kara and Zoë

Contents

Foreword

Intimate relationships can be complex and require a lot of ongoing work, especially for someone with Asperger's syndrome (AS)—as I, a person with AS, can certainly attest. I wish Cindy Ariel's book had existed during the early days of my marriage, because this resource has given the autism community a valuable tool that can bring great insight to all who wish to learn more about what relationships are like for people who have AS.

From the beginning, Dr. Ariel's accurate descriptions of Asperger's syndrome are extensive enough to replace such myths as the idea that people with AS are unemotional and unfeeling with the understanding that they are merely different and, therefore, are not a collection of deficits in need of remediation.

The initial pages draw readers to answer simple yet meaningful questions to help them gain greater insight concerning their partners on the autism spectrum. You will find pearls of wisdom throughout this book, as well as worksheets that lead to practical solutions for addressing issues and misunderstandings related to AS differences, such as perceived lack of empathy and possible resulting feelings of loneliness in the nonspectrum partner. The beauty of these worksheets is that they help non-AS partners get to the core of verbalizing how their AS partners' different behaviors make them feel, how this affects the relationship, and how the two, often very different, viewpoints are really just alternate sides of the same proverbial coin. Additionally, the sample exercises quantitatively and qualitatively help guide partners, both on and off the autism spectrum, in formulating their responses.

Another unusual and welcome aspect of this book is that *both* relationship partners can use it, working together to mutually understand one another. For example, the reframing exercises, in which each partner describes a behavior that is challenging to the relationship, can be an excellent tool for considering the real reason why a partner might give a monologue on a subject of special interest or offer extremely restricted restaurant choices. Whereas most people outside the autism spectrum may consider food to be the most important aspect in selecting a restaurant, perhaps for people with AS, the most important factor may be avoidance of fluorescent lights, which appear to them to mimic strobe lights. Such reframing exercises, for example, would have been a great time-saver in helping my wife and me come to a mutual understanding about why some restaurants were just intolerable for me to eat at with her or anyone else.

Yet another of the many exercises explores the reasons why you may have fallen in love with your partner, by examining where initial attractions originate and whether these aspects are still working for you in your relationship. This process can provide valuable insights to all couples who may have drifted apart over time and wish to examine what brought them together in the first place.

Additional important aspects of relationships explored include identifying and ranking respective needs on a scale from 1 to 10 to determine relative importance, which is something everyone can understand, whether or not Asperger's syndrome is a factor. Most of all, this work masterfully enables couples to identify, verbalize, and communicate their wishes, desires, fears, and needs in a way that both partners can understand, process, and do something about. Although I wish that this resource had been available during the first two decades of my marriage, I feel fortunate to benefit from it now and feel that it will be very helpful to many readers.

With its greater understanding of the AS partner, this book introduces the reader to easy-to-implement approaches and techniques that employ the AS partner's strengths rather than attempt to make him into something he is not. Some of these tools and concepts include tried-and-true approaches, such as using visual schedules and rating scales, preparing for transitions, being mindful of the importance of predictability, and making changes to routines one small step at a time—methods that can be very successful when adult versions are used.

Finally, while this book is about keeping couples together in a healthy manner, useful and comforting material is included for when you must make the decision to end your relationship, and how to do so as fairly and ethically as possible.

This book has the rare ability to act as an ambassador between people with Asperger's syndrome and people who are not on the autism spectrum. Cindy Ariel's work represents a giant leap forward in developing greater understanding in not only couples involving an AS partner but also people of all types who are engaged in intimate relationships. Throughout its pages, this book provides both partners in a couple greater understanding of the differences in the way people with AS perceive the environment, process information, and express themselves. Given the interactive nature of this book, all who want to learn more about improving intimate relationships with people on the autism spectrum should find it to be a valuable resource.

> —Stephen M. Shore, EdD
> Assistant Professor of Special Education, Adelphi University
> Internationally known author, consultant, and presenter on
> issues related to autism

Acknowledgments

My father, Carl H. Cohen (Todd), always believed that I would write a book someday. My mother, Lillian, lay dying over several months while I both wrote this book and served as her primary caregiver. Although neither of them knows that I wrote it, I did so in large part because of them.

"We are carried on the backs of all the writers who came before us" (Goldberg 2010, 102). I trust that I have added favorably to previous writing and current knowledge by synthesizing information in a way that presents useful ideas and constructive ways to apply them. Many past and current writers, thinkers, and researchers, in addition to the many other people I've mentioned throughout, have influenced my clinical work. I especially want to thank Simon Baron-Cohen for being so open with his work and for allowing permission to use it to help others, and Stephen M. Shore for support and help during the entire process.

Thanks to Angela Autry Gorden of New Harbinger Publications for reaching out to me and working with me in the initial stages. Editors Melissa Kirk, Jess Beebe, Nicola Skidmore, and Nelda Street expertly continued what Angela started, and worked diligently and patiently with me in shaping the final manuscript.

I would like to thank my colleagues at Alternative Choices—Kate Altman, Elise Gaul, Innessa Manevich, and Kelly Peters—who picked up the slack while I spent hours writing with my door open only an inch for really important interruptions and who were patient with my need to reschedule many meetings. Notably, the great energy and insight Innessa brings to our practice further allowed me to spend time writing relatively worry free. Toward the end of the process, Elizabeth McGarry spent several internship hours at Alternative Choices helping me with some last-minute fact checking and research, which I very much appreciated. A special thanks also goes out to the many people diagnosed on the spectrum (officially and unofficially) or in a relationship with someone on the spectrum who offered their own stories and struggles, and teach me more every day about love and life.

By far, the most support for this project came from my colleague and life partner, Robert Naseef, who not only helped edit and discuss various parts of the book but also gave me the personal and professional space I needed to write it. In doing so, he showed phenomenal love, patience, and encouragement. I also want to acknowledge my deep gratitude to Antoinette and Tariq Naseef for being significant personal teachers about the depth and breadth of love and relationships. Finally, a very thankful shout-out to my daughters, Kara and Zoë, wonderful young women who constantly inspire me to be the best I can be. Through them, my experience of love and understanding has grown exponentially.

Introduction

There is always some madness in love. But there is also always some reason in madness.

—Friedrich Nietzsche

Once upon a time, you met the person of your dreams—or maybe it just seemed like a good match. You spent time together, dated, and perhaps fell in love. Finally, you married or established a committed relationship. Now things are not quite the way you had planned.

Although partners with Asperger's syndrome (AS) may not show love in the way that you expect, they can still be very loving and loyal. You may now find yourself searching for help to keep your sanity and relationship intact, and this book was written to help you do just that. There are reasons, both conscious and unconscious, why you chose your partner, and this book will help you to explore them and reaffirm your relationship commitment.

When Your Partner Has Asperger's Syndrome

You may have discovered that the love of your life has Asperger's through a process of confusion and disappointments. This is not uncommon. You put your partner's needs before your own, and often he doesn't realize or appreciate all that you do. Your partner doesn't seem to recognize your feelings. You begin wondering why he is late or how he forgot an important event—again. You can't quite believe that your partner obliviously looks on while you struggle with a task with which you clearly need help. Your hints for help or intimacy go unacknowledged.

At this point, you may feel rejected, angry, or alone, which can lead to increasing frustration between the two of you. It feels bad to be perceived as critical or blaming, but the defensiveness and anger may continue to increase, leading you to feel invalidated and even tricked. You might be too angry to notice or care that your partner struggles with similar negative feelings. The cycle can be very painful for both of you.

The strong initial feelings of being in love often carry us through rough spots in our relationships. We selectively pay attention to positive behaviors and emotions, sometimes for a very long time. As we get to know our partners, we increasingly learn about their more difficult or challenging characteristics. You may be experiencing this now. Loving partners often work for years at trying to figure out what to do or say differently to get their partners with AS to understand how certain behaviors and attitudes affect them. You may no longer feel able to overlook many of the difficulties Asperger's syndrome poses for your intimate relationship.

Your relationship may have changed over time as your awareness of problems gradually unfolded. You may notice more and more that your partner behaves or reacts differently than past partners did. Perhaps your partner does not seem able to give you what you need on certain important levels. Her social and emotional needs may be very different from yours. You might have suspected that something was wrong, but may not have understood how deeply it would affect your relationship.

You may simply be looking for information to help you understand your partner better. Perhaps disappointment now colors your relationship, and you struggle to see the good points. Maybe you experience some of the following issues:

* You cannot rely on your partner to get chores done around the house.

* Your partner forgets to pay bills on time.

* Your partner cannot seem to get the children where they need to go.

* You cannot depend on your partner to be there for you when you feel sick.

* Your partner won't act even mildly appreciative toward your parents for lending you money.

* Your partner is between jobs again.

Such issues can result in a great deal of hurt and misunderstanding in "mixed" relationships, in other words, relationships between someone who has AS and someone who does not. In the worst-case scenario, you may be considering ending your relationship. People do not often stay in a disappointing relationship without love and a deep commitment.

What's Next?

Asperger's syndrome makes it difficult for your partner to learn some of the necessary interpersonal skills needed for a successful intimate relationship. In strong couples, each person helps the other by offering strengths to balance the other's weaknesses. If your partner excels at logic and creative solutions to household problems but these things challenge you, your partner can be your guide in these areas. If your strength lies in other relationship skills, such as expressing emotions or making small talk at parties, then you can lead by example and guide your partner. You can get more of what you want from your AS partner, but you'll have to learn new ways to ask for it.

You have come to the right place to explore what you may, at times, experience as heaviness in your relationship and your questions about how you can fix it. When you have a partner with Asperger's, you must learn to cope with the characteristics of AS for both your own sanity and the good of the relationship. It will help if you can see the world as much as possible from your partner's point of view.

Working Together

Actively involving your partner in trying to better your relationship will make it easier, although by no means easy, to progress. To work with your partner most constructively, it's essential not to view him as if he alone causes problems in your relationship. The true problems lie in the blending of two different modes of being. It is not your partner's fault that he doesn't understand certain social expectations, just as it is not your fault that you don't understand how the pipes in your house work. You are empathic, caring, and nurturing, which is why you are reading this book. If you can get your partner to read it too, that would be ideal. Your partner with AS can use his cognitive and logical strengths to help your relationship work out.

Working Alone

For many reasons, your partner may not be actively involved in working on your relationship with you. In that case, you will have to work alone. Your partner will gradually follow, and if not, her inability or unwillingness will help you to see the limitations of what can and cannot be done. Regardless, you can make changes and be more satisfied with your relationship and your life. You will need to examine your own thoughts, feelings, behaviors, and motivations in order to make changes and progress. Going it alone is harder but doable.

Keeping a Journal

Writing in a journal helps many people to get some of their ideas and feelings out. It also helps to work through difficult issues privately and in your own time. Writing translates feelings into words and can be helpful for discovering your innermost thoughts and enhancing your perspective. Rather than repeatedly write about the same upsetting situations, look for new realizations and ideas to write about.

Each of the following chapters in this book will offer you some journal-keeping suggestions to help get you started. For now, get a notebook to use as your journal and set aside ten to fifteen minutes to complete the following sentences:

* *The best thing about my partner is* _____.

* *I cannot stand when my partner* _____.

* *My hope for our relationship is* _____.

Not everyone likes keeping a journal. While writing may be a great way for you to work out thoughts and feelings, you or your partner may prefer to reflect on these ideas another way. You can choose to give yourself time for reflection that does not involve keeping a journal. If you do this, be aware that you will get the most out of the exercise if you truly set aside the required ten to fifteen minutes to reflect. Taking notes would also be helpful, and your notes don't have to become an official journal.

Getting Started

Throughout this book, you will gain insight, understanding, and help to focus on improving and enjoying your relationship. The skills and information you learn apply whether your partner is the same or opposite sex. We will start by exploring Asperger's syndrome itself and how you ended up with a partner who has the characteristic strengths and relationship difficulties of someone with AS. Then we will delve into the disillusionment and anger that you may feel, and the intense emotional deprivation that you may sometimes experience. We will consider ways to face many issues that cause dissatisfaction and to make significant changes. Some specific topics of exploration include:

* Obsessions or special interests

* Embarrassment over grooming habits

* Socializing as a couple

* Organizational skills and problems

* Meltdowns and anger management

* Communication problems and difficulty interacting

* Dealing with rigidity and lack of spontaneity

* Your partner's seeming lack of empathy

Throughout this book, you will learn which part of your relationship problems most likely stem from differences due to Asperger's syndrome and which issues commonly develop in any relationship. When and how to try to work on your own to improve your relationship, as well as when it may be necessary to involve a third party, will also be discussed.

You may love your partner deeply, but sometimes love is not enough to keep a relationship alive. I am hopeful that you have enough energy left to focus on rekindling the positive feelings of love between you and your partner. The ideas presented in this book will help you to renew your energy until, over time, your loving partnership will naturally renew you. You can work to understand what stands between you and your partner. I hope to help the two of you to live together in a happy and fulfilling relationship.

CHAPTER 1

Asperger's Syndrome

Whenever you find yourself on the side of the
majority, it is time to pause and reflect.

—Mark Twain

Your partner is not part of the majority. The first step in improving your relationship involves learning as much as you can about Asperger's syndrome. Intimate partnerships combine two separate personalities, plus the various backgrounds and experiences that each brings. Your relationship contains an added challenge, because you and your AS partner think and feel very differently. You both must learn to relate differently, and understanding a different perspective or learning new ways of relating comes much easier for you, especially in intimate matters.

Does your partner seem to appreciate solitude more than togetherness? Does he sometimes smile at you with a twinkle in his eye yet seem to have no idea what you need from him? Is your partner brilliant yet seems to lack common sense? Can he be loyal and wonderful, yet totally rude? If your partner is male, is this behavior more than typical male cluelessness? Or, if your partner is a woman, is it more than strong feminine independence?

If your partner has been diagnosed with Asperger's syndrome, you probably want to immerse yourself in learning as much as you can about the condition. Hopefully, your partner can also accept her condition and its role in your relationship. Your happiness and satisfaction together can increase when you learn to use your understanding of AS to effectively work on improving your relationship.

The behavior of people with Asperger's can be hard to understand. Learning about this condition can help you reach new levels of compassion for yourself and your partner. Even if you believe that your partner has AS but he has not been officially diagnosed, you can benefit from the information and tools in this book, beginning with a brief primer on Asperger's syndrome itself.

The Autism Spectrum

Asperger's syndrome makes up part of a larger category of conditions called *autism spectrum disorders* (ASDs), or autism spectrum conditions. These conditions are also currently known as *pervasive developmental disorders* (PDDs). "Pervasive" means that the challenges can affect many abilities, from social to academic learning, and physical mannerisms. Asperger's can also include widespread difficulties in taking in, organizing, and understanding information. People with AS can be physically as well as socially awkward, use unusual speech patterns, show hypersensitivity to certain sensations, and so on. Asperger's makes social connections harder for the brain to process. The differences are pervasive.

Autism spectrum conditions, including Asperger's syndrome, are *neurological*, meaning that they stem from variations in the brain. Development that relates to the brain is called *neurological development*. Variations in neurological development result in different brain connections that affect the way the brain works. People with Asperger's have a neurological makeup that's different from that of the majority of people, and from the typically developing brain. People with a neurologically typical brain are sometimes referred to as *neurotypical*.

Classic autism (the most severe form), *high-functioning autism*, and Asperger's syndrome result in different levels of functioning. Intellectual abilities in people with autism conditions range from severely impaired to superior. In Asperger's syndrome, the person's IQ typically meets at least the average range of intelligence, and many people with AS actually perform much higher. Due to this and other areas of diversity, autism is considered a spectrum condition: a wide range of ability and disability exists in people on the autism spectrum.

Asperger's Syndrome and Autism

The term "Asperger's syndrome" is often used interchangeably with "high-functioning autism." The difference in official diagnosis has to do with the early development of language and the absence of early cognitive delays. Autism usually causes some type of language delay, and some people with classic autism never learn to speak at all. In contrast, people with Asperger's frequently have good language skills, although they may use language in unique ways. For example, their speech might sound overly formal or may be repetitive, resulting in their asking the same question over and over.

As with all autism spectrum conditions, Asperger's leads to significant struggles in social interaction, frequently coupled with limited interests and repetitive behaviors. In general, the difficulties seen in Asperger's syndrome appear milder than in autism. People with classic autism often seem to prefer solitary activities. People with AS frequently want relationships but possess limited or unclear understanding of how to make positive social connections.

A Brief History

To better understand your situation, consider some background information regarding Asperger's syndrome. The term "autism" was first used to refer to the intense self-absorption seen in schizophrenic patients. Over time, understanding grew that autism and schizophrenia represent different conditions.

In the early 1940s, Dr. Leo Kanner (1943), of Johns Hopkins University, used the term "autism" to describe children with severe limitations in communication and social interaction. Around the same time, Hans Asperger ([1944] 1991), an Austrian pediatrician, wrote a paper in German about autism as well. Asperger described a condition that coupled "autistic" behaviors with certain characteristic strengths. Researchers and medical professionals working to understand autism and Asperger's syndrome realize now that the two terms represent different variations on a theme; they seem to exist on a continuum or spectrum.

Changes in Diagnosis

Medical and mental health professionals use the *Diagnostic and Statistical Manual of Mental Disorders* (*DSM*) as an official guide for diagnosing mental disorders and syndromes. Asperger's work slowly became more widely known in the United States once his original paper was translated from German into English in 1991. Asperger's syndrome was officially listed in the fourth edition (American Psychiatric Association 1994) of the *DSM*, the *DSM-IV*. Only the more severe cases of autism were likely detected in the educational and mental health systems before that point. Many people with Asperger's syndrome, quite possibly including your partner, remain undiagnosed.

When the *DSM* text was revised in 2000 (*DSM-IV-TR*), Asperger's syndrome remained as a pervasive developmental disorder. With the release of the next edition of the *DSM* in 2013, the *DSM-V*, what we now understand as pervasive developmental disorders will fall under one large category of autism spectrum disorders. The diagnosis of Asperger's syndrome will officially become autism spectrum disorder.

For various reasons, including old stereotypes linking autism with schizophrenia and intellectual disability, and the broad ranges of behavior seen on the autism spectrum, some people disagree with combining these diagnoses. However, many professionals working closely with people who have AS, and many adults diagnosed with either AS or high-functioning autism, believe that the change will ultimately be a positive one. Hopefully, any changes made in the diagnostic process will improve our understanding of all people on the autism spectrum and help professionals to meet their diverse needs.

The Biology

Researchers continue to investigate the causes of Asperger's syndrome. Currently they believe the condition is caused by a combination of genes and the environment (Newschaffer et al. 2007). Environmental factors are thought to contribute to autism spectrum conditions, although studies have not made clear and consistent links. Differences in the brains of people with Asperger's syndrome help us to understand the biology of this complicated condition.

The Asperger's Brain

Brain scans show differences in shape and structure of the brain of the person with Asperger's syndrome compared to the brain of a person without AS (DiCicco-Bloom et al. 2006). Beginning in the womb, the growth and development of the brain affects its wiring and connections. Someone with Asperger's doesn't process information in the same way as someone with a neurotypical brain. The AS brain may not necessarily make certain connections automatically. For example, there is often extreme difficulty reading faces or picking up on nonverbal cues that are important to social communication. The brain of someone with Asperger's syndrome may not connect a common expression with a specific feeling in the same way that yours does. These differences affect your AS partner's life and how she experiences and understands the world.

Genetic Factors

All autism spectrum conditions, including Asperger's syndrome, have a strong genetic component, which means that they run in families. No specific gene has been identified for Asperger's, and studies suggest that variations in many different genes may lead the fetus to develop autism (National Institutes of Health 2009). Families with one child diagnosed with Asperger's often have other children with either a diagnosis on the autism spectrum or related conditions, such as learning disabilities or delays in speech development, a fact that also points to the genetic nature of this condition (Boyle, van Naarden Braun, and Yeargin-Allsopp 2005). The rate at which a diagnosed child's siblings will also have autism-related conditions has been shown to be much higher in twins (ibid.).

Males vs. Females

Most people diagnosed with Asperger's syndrome are male. Based on a major research article, the website of the Centers for Disease Control and Prevention (CDC) (2011) reports that the ratio of men to women with this condition is four or five to one. This means that right now, on average, for every four or five men diagnosed with Asperger's syndrome, there is one woman diagnosed with the syndrome as well.

Several theories explain why the difference exists, including the idea that women are generally better at socializing than men and don't call attention to their social or emotional needs in the same ways. Girls are also typically socialized differently, with different expectations, which might leave girls and women under the radar of the official diagnosis more often than boys and men. In addition, hyperactivity and aggression in males may gain the attention of professionals more than the usually less aggressive, more cooperative girls. Different gender expectations may actually help girls with Asperger's to work harder in social situations and learn to "pass" as typical more than boys can. While more boys than girls are diagnosed with AS, so far research is unclear as to whether this means that there are actually fewer females with the condition or that girls and women are drastically underdiagnosed and misdiagnosed.

Women with AS may still have unusual physical movement, obsessive interests, and difficulty understanding complicated social interaction and communication. Whether your partner is male or female, both of you may be frustrated with social and emotional difficulties related to Asperger's syndrome.

Living with Asperger's

While some people with Asperger's learn to fit in, others remain isolated due to severe difficulties in social and work situations. Even in people who learn to appear typical, AS presents many problems. Overall, many people with Asperger's syndrome can function well in their day-to-day world by highlighting their strengths and compensating for weaknesses. A common profile of people with AS shows men and women who:

*   Often have career success, although other impairments can limit achievements

*   May seem brilliant yet quirky

*   Demonstrate intense attachment to hobbies or interests (computers, train schedules, mathematics, music, and so on)

*   Develop low self-esteem and lack self-confidence from being frequently misunderstood in school, jobs, and relationships

*   Struggle in intimate relationships

Asperger's can be less noticeable in adulthood than in childhood, because some people can learn to compensate for symptoms and unusual behaviors. However, certain symptoms can be even more pronounced, because situations in adulthood may call for higher levels of appropriate and expected social interaction. For example, by the time a person with AS begins dating or holding a job, his brilliance may not be enough to carry him through. In fact, it becomes even harder for others to understand him. He may not initiate phone conversations, socialize appropriately at events, or interact with coworkers when necessary.

How can someone so brilliant not realize when he behaves rudely or that you need him to do more around the house? While your partner has many strengths and characteristics that attracted you, some of his primary weaknesses may be highlighted as a result of your relationship.

A common misperception about people with Asperger's syndrome is that they are uncaring and do not like people. People with AS can be very sensitive to others, and some can be quite emotional at times. The difference lies in the way caring and concern are experienced and expressed. Also, while someone with AS may want to enjoy various relationships, it can be frustrating for her to understand the many unwritten rules of social behavior.

The Asperger's Advantage

As yet, there is no cure for Asperger's syndrome, and many people would not want one. The high-functioning autism profile offers abilities and strengths that help people with AS to excel in certain positions compared to many neurotypical peers. Hans Asperger (1979) referred to these advantages in his oft-quoted suggestion that "for success in science and art, a dash of autism is essential."

Many people diagnosed with Asperger's syndrome, as well as professionals who work with them, consider the condition to be more like another culture or way of being than a disability. The following list presents some of the AS advantages. How many of them does your partner demonstrate?

* High or superior IQ

* Excellent memory for certain facts and details

* Intense focus and attentiveness

* Steadfast loyalty

* Strong sense of justice

* Nonconformist attitudes

* Clear moral beliefs

* Kind and gentle behavior

* Extensive vocabulary

* Creative talent

Several of these advantages can sometimes translate into obsessions or unrealistically high standards. Nevertheless, people with Asperger's syndrome often demonstrate exceptional abilities in their chosen fields because of their intense focus, dependability, and intelligence. Less time socializing can also lead to more time focusing on practical matters, such as improving the speed of your laptop computer or rewiring your home electrical system.

EXERCISE 1.1   AS Advantages in Your Relationship

Your partner brings many positive traits to the table. Improving your relationship involves highlighting these traits and using them to make needed changes. This exercise focuses on the positive characteristics of Asperger's in your relationship. The sample exercise, "My Partner's AS Advantages," will help you to begin.

1. List at least three positive attributes your partner offers in your relationship. Resist the urge to add how any of them may have also become a negative trait. For now, just give your partner credit for positive characteristics.

2. Write a sentence or two next to each item in the list to explain how this trait positively affects your relationship.

3. Keep this list handy to refer to later. Your partner's positive traits may be useful in strengthening weaker areas of relating. Rereading the list at times can also remind you of the positive characteristics that help to make your relationship worth your continued love and energy.

SAMPLE EXERCISE 1.1
My Partner's AS Advantages

Intensely focused	Persistent until he fixes what breaks around the house. Can learn to fix almost anything.
Honest	I can trust that whatever he tells me is truthful.
Calm	Does not become easily upset or stressed by things not working around the house; he just goes about fixing them.
Predictable	I can rely on him to do exactly what he says he will do, when he says he will do it.

Your partner may not have the same positive attributes as the one in this example. People with AS can demonstrate different traits and abilities. Think about your partner's unique, positive traits as you work on your own chart.

Asperger's Syndrome: Ability or Disability?

What we commonly refer to as Asperger's syndrome falls under the official heading "Asperger's Disorder" in the *DSM-IV-TR* (APA 2000). There remains controversy over whether AS constitutes a disorder. Does being different make you disordered?

Many professionals in the field consider Asperger's to be a clear example of *neurodiversity*; brains have different abilities, and being different is not the same as having a disability. Neurodiversity suggests that we should acknowledge and appreciate other ways of processing information and making sense of the world beyond the typical ways of thinking and behaving.

Certain AS challenges can be debilitating for some people. Behaviors and thinking patterns of people with Asperger's syndrome often lead to rejection in all kinds of relationships. At the same time, the AS advantages can balance out and even outweigh the challenges for many people with AS. Neurodiversity reminds us that there's more than one right way to understand and interact with others.

What Asperger's Means for You

If your partner has Asperger's syndrome, real, internal neurological differences exist between her brain and yours. It helps to take these differences into account when you consider your partner's behavior in your relationship. Neurological differences do not change significantly over time. However, people with neurological differences can learn to compensate for unusual behavior. Clearly communicating your expectations to your partner can be useful in improving your relationship.

Certain personality characteristics can accompany Asperger's syndrome, though they are not a part of the AS diagnosis (see chapter 11 for information on conditions that commonly coexist with AS). For example, social awkwardness or lack of eye contact can make some people appear arrogant or narcissistic. But arrogance and narcissism are not an inevitable part of Asperger's.

The person with AS often does not realize how others interpret these behaviors, but he can learn to take others' expectations and interpretations into account. So while a lack of understanding of social cues may stem from your partner's neurological makeup, he can learn to change his outward appearance and behavior. He can learn the importance of eye contact, a social smile, or postures that appear friendlier or less awkward. Your partner can learn to be better at meeting your expectations, and you can be an important part of the process.

Points to Keep in Mind

Many characteristics of Asperger's syndrome may lead you to question your relationship. The more you can see that the natural differences between you and your partner stem from differences in neurological makeup, the more you can learn to speak the same language of love.

With more information comes hope; now that you know the situation, you can do something about it. Even if your partner will not initially work with you toward change, your relationship and how you feel about it can improve. In reading this book, you will gain insights that help you regain hope and begin to change the chemistry in your relationship.

The next chapter discusses more specifically the ways that Asperger's syndrome might affect your intimate partnership and result in potential unmet needs and expectations. Later, the book deals with how you got here in the first place, and how to get what you need and deserve in your relationship.

CHAPTER 2

Asperger's Syndrome and Relationships

In true love, the smallest distance is too great,
and the greatest distance can be bridged.

—Hans Nouwens

All relationships take patience, hard work, and understanding. Relationships in which one partner has Asperger's syndrome contain additional obstacles, and the virtues of hard work, patience, and understanding sometimes need to be present in overabundance. Limited social understanding, coupled with other challenges, such as organizational difficulties or black-and-white thinking, strongly affects relationships in which one partner has AS. Still, while sometimes fraught with disappointment and frustration, your relationship has the potential for a strong bond of love and commitment that makes it worth working for.

Pretending to Be "Normal"

Liane Holliday Willey wrote an autobiographical account of her life with autism, called *Pretending to Be Normal: Living with Asperger's Syndrome* (1999). I often hear these or similar words expressed in counseling sessions. There are many different types of people with AS: some tend to be more emotionally sensitive, while others appear to be more practical, logical, or rule driven. In any case, people eventually diagnosed with AS often describe themselves as "pretending to be normal."

Many people develop strategies to compensate for their social difficulties, but not everyone with AS can appear to be typical. Some fit in well in some situations but not in others, while some people have difficulty fitting in at all. Either way, adapting in social situations can take an overwhelming amount of energy for someone with Asperger's. Your partner may enjoy socializing at times, although doing so may present great personal challenges.

How Asperger's Affects Relationships

Someone diagnosed with Asperger's syndrome typically demonstrates problems in two main areas: social interaction and patterns of behavior, interests, and activities. These and other issues become pervasive in the intimate relationships of people with AS.

Social Interaction

People with Asperger's syndrome often demonstrate socially awkward behavior and interaction. They may carry on an intelligent conversation but not know how to initiate or end one. Leslie gives one-word answers when asked about her day, such as "Fine" or "Boring." Having to "pull teeth" to get more information frustrates her partner, who feels particularly embarrassed around family and friends when Leslie seems withdrawn. Another person with AS may be hard to stop after starting a conversation.

Interaction that requires give-and-take, such as listening and sharing information, may not come naturally to someone with Asperger's syndrome. He may need prompting to carry on a mutual conversation, which may stop and start rather than flow smoothly. Conversations can also be one sided if your AS partner gets to talking about his special interest. Charlie talks about his racehorses, whether people show interest or not. It's one of his favorite topics, so he assumes everyone else is interested as well. Such traits can make people with AS seem rude and clueless.

Each person with Asperger's syndrome is unique, although many share certain tendencies. Of the various "Aspergian" traits, your partner may have any number or combination. Here are a few ways that your partner with AS might express difficulties with social interaction in your relationship. Does your partner tend to have any of the following traits?

*   Looks down or away when speaking

*   Ignores or misunderstands nonverbal cues or body language

*   Has trouble expressing or managing feelings

*   Shows confusion as to the importance or purpose of positive feedback

*   Finds emotions confusing or uninteresting

*   Seems unaware of the feelings or perceptions of others

Your partner's difficulty with social interaction may make her seem uninterested in relating to others. Mary, who has Asperger's syndrome, declines invitations for Sunday brunch, because taking quiet time to do the *New York Times* crossword comforts her. This type of behavior isolates and frustrates Mary's partner and becomes a focus of our therapy sessions. Without a resolution, this issue may become more problematic over time, as the two partners drift farther apart and become more isolated from others. In this particular case, Mary agreed that her partner could plan a relationship activity for Sunday afternoons, as long as she could have her Sunday mornings alone.

It can be hard for someone with AS to hold himself together socially out in the world and have to relate on an almost constant basis at home too. When Lou gets home from work, he wants to read his favorite blogs, so he becomes very moody if approached, because he needs this time to recharge from his day. This causes many arguments with his partner, who feels that Lou should spend "couple" time after their being apart all day. Both partners have a valid viewpoint, so we look for compromises in our work together. You may need to do much work to help yourself get the interaction you need from your partner. On the other hand, your partner may need support to get the alone time he needs, to feel more comfortable in other settings when possible, and to understand your social value system.

Language and Communication

Although language can be a strength for people with Asperger's syndrome, problems with social communication and interpretation of language occur commonly. People with AS may have problems with subtle aspects of social communication, such as nonverbal body language or certain types of humor, such as sarcasm. These traits make it difficult for others to understand someone with AS, and often result in the exclusion or rejection of the person.

Language and communication problems in Asperger's syndrome can affect relationships in significant ways. How often does your partner do the following?

* Maintain too much or too little personal space when talking to others

* Interpret the things you say literally

* Have difficulty maintaining conversation

* Misunderstand your jokes

Communication problems can develop in your relationship from verbal and nonverbal misunderstandings. For example, when you feel upset, your partner may not get it and may walk away, assuming that you need time alone to get yourself under control. When your partner feels overwhelmed, time alone to regroup may typically work for her. If she knew that rather than alone time, you need for her to sit with you and offer reassurance, she could learn to do this, even though it might not automatically cross her mind.

Unusual Behavior and Obsessive Interests

Repetitive or focused activities represent another feature of Asperger's syndrome. Someone with AS may focus obsessively on a single topic—his special interest—and talk about it to the exclusion of other topics. To add to this annoyance, the person's difficulty in seeing another perspective makes it hard for him to understand that others may interpret his singular focus as boring or inappropriate.

Repeated routines and uncoordinated movement often mark someone with Asperger's syndrome. Common movements, such as rocking, fidgeting, or pacing, usually don't interfere with relationships, but do sometimes concern partners when they see these behaviors become more frequent. Stress and anxiety can cause this to happen, and your partner may need your support to notice and help decrease stress when these behaviors rise to an uncomfortable level.

Unusual interests and repetitive behaviors may also affect relationships. Which of the following have you noticed in your partner?

* Highly focused special interests

* Special interests that interfere with other activities

* Preference for repetitive routines

* Discomfort with spontaneity

* Inflexibility or black-and-white thinking

* Tendency to get easily upset by change

Sometimes the intensity of a special interest may not seem unusual, but the topic does. For example, Teagan may only spend a few moments checking out the door hinges wherever she goes, but this type of preoccupation is unusual.

The intensity of your partner's special interests can influence you to lose interest in something you previously enjoyed. In determining how to get your needs met (chapter 5), you can set goals to regain an appreciation of your own lost interests, or develop interests together as a couple. Use your partner's interests to find a new activity that you both enjoy. Remember that your partner's brain is wired to enjoy focused attention.

Goals for improving your relationship can include setting aside time to focus on your partner's special interest and time to focus on other things together.

EXERCISE 2.1   Asperger's in Your Relationship

Let's explore ways in which the two main areas of difficulty in Asperger's syndrome affect your relationship. The sample exercise, "Asperger's in Our Relationship," will help you get started on this exercise.

1. On a sheet of paper or in your journal, make two headings, "Social Interaction" and "Unusual Behavior and Obsessive Interests."

2. Under each heading, list ways in which these two areas cause problems for you.

3. With each item on the list, write a sentence or two about how it affects you or your relationship.

SAMPLE EXERCISE 2.1
Asperger's in Our Relationship

Social Interaction	Unusual Behavior and Obsessive Interests
He doesn't talk in the car. I feel rejected and lonely.	He talks about animals constantly. He's so self-absorbed; he doesn't know me.
He rarely looks at me when we talk. I can't tell if he pays attention or understands me.	He has to smell anything he eats or buys. It embarrasses me when he smells clothes before buying.
He goes to our room when he gets home, without saying hello. I feel ignored and lonely, as if I don't have a partner.	He's on the computer more than he is with anyone, including me. I think he loves the computer more than me. I feel like smashing it.

This exercise helps you to start looking at how AS affects your relationship. As we go on, it will help you to understand how some common issues in your relationship develop from AS, rather than as a result of the failures or weaknesses of you or your partner. Seeing relationship issues as part of Asperger's syndrome helps couples stop blaming each other and start working together in more rewarding and loving ways.

Relationship Challenges

Differences in ways of thinking and experiencing the world between neurotypical partners and partners with Asperger's lead to several common areas of distress in relationships. Differences in social interaction, along with unusual behaviors and obsessive interests, are at the root of many relationship difficulties. Problems can be sparked by a seeming lack of compassion, heightened sensitivities, and difficulties with organization. Verbal and nonverbal misunderstandings create problems too.

Differing Perspectives

You and your partner probably see many of each other's behaviors and interactions from different perspectives. Consider the differences shown in the following table.

TABLE 2.1 Differences in Perspective

Different way of viewing...	Partner with AS sees it as...	Non-AS partner sees it as...
Eye contact	Pointless, meaningless, overwhelming	Reflecting honesty, concern, attentiveness
Flexibility	Chaotic, illogical	Fun, spontaneous
Predictability	Easy to manage	Boring

Small talk	Meaningless	An icebreaker, something that builds relationship
Solitude	Peaceful, calming	Lonely, distancing
Asking for what you want	Essential ("How else can I know?")	Something intuitive ("My partner should just 'know'")

Differences such as these contribute to common difficulties for people with Asperger's syndrome. They make up part of the "hidden curriculum" in your relationship: the unstated rules that you may understand, but that your AS partner may not be able to pick up as easily (Smith Myles, Trautman, and Schelvan 2004). For people with AS who are trying to navigate an intimate relationship, these unstated rules create many challenges and misunderstandings. We will explore their various day-to-day effects in intimate relationships and coping strategies to help you deal with them.

Decision Making

People with Asperger's tend to think logically and may not allow emotions to cloud rational decision making. Partners with AS often have a strong interest in maintaining things a certain way, and can be very strong and persistent about it. They often develop logical explanations that make total sense to them, but may confuse you or make no sense to you at all.

Your partner may make unilateral decisions based on her need for predictability or in a misguided attempt to please you. Sylvia wiped out the joint bank account to purchase an amazing car that her partner had expressed an interest in. At other times, your partner may stay uninvolved in decisions because she feels uncertain of what to do or has no interest in the outcome. A couple that came to me for counseling argued over the fact that Ray would not help Sam pick out a new car. Ray had more experience and knowledge about cars but didn't drive to work, so he showed no interest in helping Sam choose a car. Ray was willing to help once he understood the logic of Sam's request.

Sometimes your partner may withdraw from the decision-making process because it seems complicated and overwhelming. For instance, for Bobbie to get involved in working with her partner to refinance the house, she would spend unlimited amounts of time researching banks, lenders, and interest rates, and otherwise getting lost in details. She wanted to do the right thing, but decision making includes a lot of potential for error. At such times in your own relationship, you may feel burdened by having to be the sole decision maker.

COPING STRATEGIES FOR DECISION MAKING

Your partner may be more likely to respond to your ideas if you present them rationally and logically. Flowcharts provide step-by-step guidance for making decisions and can help your partner to follow your idea in a logical sequence, which is how Bobbie's partner made the decision-making process less overwhelming to her. The next chapter (chapter 3) provides an example of a flowchart and how to develop one, along with a step-by-step model for decision making. Chapter 7 covers how to present ideas in a rational and logical way that your partner with AS may be more likely to respond to.

Inflexibility and Rigidity

A partner's rigidity and lack of spontaneity often becomes a flash point or area of disappointment in intimate relationships. People with Asperger's syndrome are often known to have inflexible thought patterns, seeing things as all or nothing, black-and-white without gray in between. Such rigid thinking tends to make new ideas and planning difficult. Any change in daily routine can be extremely difficult for your partner to tolerate.

Unpredictability can lead to a feeling of losing control. Your partner's rigidity may sometimes have to do with his need to manage his environment to deal with the anxiety or hypersensitivity that can accompany AS. Such issues can lead him to be inflexible about what he eats, where he goes, and how he spends his time. Many people with Asperger's have difficulty handling the intrusion of intimate relationships. AS partners sometimes feel that they must either quit their jobs or end the relationship in order to succeed in at least one of those areas.

COPING STRATEGIES FOR INFLEXIBILITY
AND RIGIDITY

Unexpected changes can cause high levels of stress and anxiety. Include your partner in any decisions about changes regarding household or relationship routines, events, and expectations. When this isn't possible, try to notify your partner in advance of upcoming changes.

If your partner agrees, you can help her practice flexible thinking and become better at it. Remind your partner about shades of gray whenever an opportunity arises. Offer more than one reason why something can happen or why someone might behave in a certain way. Your partner may even agree for you to surprise her once or twice a week. These "surprises" may have to start very small to help your partner slowly break out of rigid patterns. You can change what you usually make for dinner or the way you prepare it. The possibility of increased flexibility improves with change that comes about deliberately and thoughtfully.

You can change things, but do it ever so slowly, and in the meantime take care of yourself. If you get tired of rarely dining out or of going to the same few places, make arrangements to go out with a friend and pick a new place to try. You may prefer to go with your partner, but it's sometimes better to go with someone else than not at all.

Organization

People with Asperger's syndrome often have difficulty with *executive functioning*, which includes the ability to organize and remember tasks. AS partners tend either to be unorganized and have trouble getting things together, or to be rigidly organized and become upset with changes in their organizational systems. Joe, who has AS, explains that when his partner tries to be helpful by straightening up his desk, it contradicts his own organizational methods. He then spends the next hour reorganizing his desktop and possibly all of the drawers to make sure he knows where everything is. I worked with Joe's non-AS partner to help her to be less "helpful" in this way.

Household management can suffer due to your partner's potential issues with short-term memory and disorganization. The division of labor may become more and more unequal because your partner does not perform certain chores to your standard or forgets altogether. One partner complained that his AS wife washed only the inside of the mugs and glasses, even after he had repeatedly pointed out that the outside also needs washing. Responsibility overload may become an area of dissatisfaction in your relationship, with resentment building on both sides. You may feel that you cannot depend on your partner to help you when necessary, while she may resent being treated like a child.

Executive-functioning difficulties can be hard to understand, because the person with AS may otherwise be extremely intelligent and capable of performing many tasks. The fact that your partner is well educated and knowledgeable in his field may confuse you when he cannot maintain employment, perform household responsibilities, or even hold an intimate conversation. Your partner may seem lazy, unmotivated, or manipulative, but he really may need support in handling life's demands.

COPING STRATEGIES FOR ORGANIZATION

Your partner may need visual support and structure to plan and carry out certain responsibilities. It may take a good bit of persistence and creativity to get what you want from your partner and feel good about it. Chapters 3 and 7 offer information about using visual aids, such as calendars, checklists, and written reminders, to help your partner with memory and organization, along with examples of chore charts and other communication tools.

Relationships with Friends and Family

The lack of social understanding and the unusual social presentation that can be the trademark of an AS partner may also affect your relationships with family and friends. Your partner can be clueless that her grooming habits embarrass you or communicate an uncaring attitude to you and those around you. Your partner's quirky, honest-to-a-fault, nonconformist attitude, which originally impressed you, can become a source of embarrassment. She may be unintentionally offensive to friends, family, and coworkers.

Even when you inform your partner about her offenses, she may arrogantly disagree. Margie was appalled that time and time again, Ronnie looked disheveled when he picked her up from work, embarrassing her in front of her colleagues. Ronnie couldn't care less about what people he didn't know thought about how he looked. He thought it made no sense when Margie spent an hour getting ready to go shopping in order to look nice for strangers.

People with Asperger's syndrome don't necessarily try to please others, because this may not seem rational from their point of view. Why try to please people you do not know? One woman complained that her partner wouldn't say hello to her friends and would walk away when the couple ran into them at the market. He responded rationally that he didn't know them, so why should he stand there while she chatted with strangers? Another partner's husband with AS went to a family dinner in pajamas. His logic was that it was only family; he worked all week and wanted to be comfortable. Non-AS partners often complain of the resentment and embarrassment that these situations cause them.

In addition, AS logic can be quite literal. Your partner may logically assume that if you ask her a question, you want her honest answer. If asked, she may tell your mother that her new dress or hairstyle for the evening's special occasion is unflattering. Your partner may have an interest in relationships but lack understanding of social conventions. It can take a while for someone with AS to learn nuanced rules regarding diplomacy or discretion versus honesty in social settings. It may sometimes be hard to explain your partner to family and friends.

COPING STRATEGIES FOR RELATIONSHIPS WITH FRIENDS AND FAMILY

While you might see good grooming or social diplomacy as common sense, this may not connect logically for your partner. He might be more willing to change his behavior in this regard if he knew how important this was to you. Your partner may never feel a need to brush his hair before leaving the house, or care about his wrinkled clothes. He can learn to brush his hair and change his pajama pants because it matters to you—and you matter to him.

Understanding your partner's social difficulties can help you to reconsider some of your expectations and support your partner so that your respective social needs and your relationship do not suffer. It's important to listen and acknowledge your partner's real difficulties. Be creative about moving forward while not pushing either of you so far outside of your comfort zone that you want to retreat. Some people with AS attend social skills courses or groups to learn behaviors that non-AS partners find important.

Sensory Issues

Sensory sensitivities often go hand in hand with Asperger's syndrome and may make your partner uncomfortable in certain situations. Places requiring a jacket and tie may be out of the question for someone who cannot stand the feel of a stiff shirt or a collar too close to the neck. The constant flickering of fluorescent bulbs in your favorite eatery may make it impossible for your partner to enjoy a meal there with you. The intensity of sensory issues can bring out increased rigidity in your partner, as he tries to avoid situations that feel intolerable to him.

COPING STRATEGIES FOR SENSORY ISSUES

When your partner complains about a new situation, try to discover whether sensory difficulties play a part. Consider lighting, room temperature, the number of people involved, the expected interaction, and other factors in overall noise and stimulation level. Chapter 11 explores conditions that often accompany AS, including heightened sensory awareness, and how to help your partner to manage them.

Now What Do You Do?

The difficulties that AS partners struggle with, in terms of social interaction, behavior, and interests, have widespread effects on your intimacy. But there are many coping strategies and ways to get through difficult situations that you can use if you focus on your partner and your specific relationship. Try not to take personally your partner's need for support in the social and behavioral arena. These issues commonly accompany Asperger's and may have little to do with you.

Your relationship can improve if you address difficult areas calmly and rationally rather than by reacting emotionally, even though you may feel upset, angry, or hurt. You will gain skills for doing so as you proceed in learning relationship tools for loving your partner with Asperger's syndrome. To begin, learning to reframe your partner's behavior will help you deal more positively with the characteristics that make you two different from each other.

Reframing

In the book written with her AS partner, Keith Newton, Sarah Hendrickx stated, "When I came from the viewpoint that he was mean and I was mistreated, nothing changed. When I reframed the picture to show that he was just seeing the world his way and that I was misunderstanding him, things improved" (Hendrickx and Newton 2007, 63). When you picture your partner as cold and uncaring, you are more likely to put a negative spin on everything he does. You can learn to take a step back from anger or other upsetting emotions, and reframe the picture of your partner's behavior. Try to look at events the way your partner may perceive them. Taking out some of the angry charge or frustration can help you to improve the way you work with your partner to get your emotional needs met.

EXERCISE 2.2   Reframing Your Partner's Behavior

This exercise helps you to be more aware of your emotional reactions and to take a different view of your partner's intentions. The sample exercise, "Reframing My Partner's Behavior," offers an idea of what your exercise should look like.

1.   Divide a sheet of paper into three columns.

2.   Label the columns "Behavior or Situation," "How It Makes Me Feel," and "Another Perspective."

3.   In the first column, describe a behavior of your partner or a relationship situation that makes you feel sad, upset, or angry. Use descriptions

only; observe and describe the event or behavior with no feeling or interpretation.

4. Write your feelings and interpretations in the second column. Include why you believe that your partner engages in these behaviors and why they hurt or frustrate you.

5. Try to think of at least one alternative reason for the behavior or situation, and write it in the third column.

SAMPLE EXERCISE 2.2

Reframing My Partner's Behavior

Behavior or Situation	How It Makes Me Feel	Another Perspective
There's only one restaurant that Sally will go to; we haven't dined anywhere else since we first met.	She doesn't think of me or what I like. She doesn't like to spend time with me in public.	She likes this place because it's quiet and serves her favorite food. She doesn't like eating in public and never did.
When I was sick in bed for three days, she came in only at dinnertime. She left food without asking how I felt.	This proves how self-centered she is. She didn't care that I felt lonely and sad because of our lack of connection.	She likes to be alone when she feels sick. She thinks asking people how they feel when they're sick is dumb.
When we go out with friends, she usually doesn't talk unless it's about stocks, and everyone gets bored.	She's rude and self-absorbed, only caring about her own interests.	Maybe she's uncertain what to say and doesn't understand cues that let her know when her topic is boring.

Separating your observations and factual descriptions of hurtful events from your assumptions and feelings about them takes practice, as does considering another perspective for such behavior. Practicing doing this can help take the edge off some lonely moments and help you to reframe your potential feelings of emotional deprivation or anger. It helps to remember that thinking something and feeling strongly about it do not make it true.

Reframing situations that cause strong emotional responses may not change the emotions you feel. Understanding your partner's behavior better doesn't mean that you agree or that you necessarily feel better after knowing your partner's logic. It just helps to take a step back and view things from another perspective. It may quell your emotions just a bit and give you the space to come up with creative solutions to get your needs met.

If you and your partner both completed the reframing exercise, spend time talking about it. Do you know what you do that makes your partner feel disconnected, and do you know how he interprets your behavior? Your partner may not complete the formal exercise, but can still share his perspective with you. If you cannot fathom another reason for your partner's "cruel" behavior, you can ask him to help you understand it. Your partner may seem quite capable in the rest of life, and you may feel that he purposely acts in certain ways, but this may be far from the case.

Relationship Warning Signs

In spite of difficulties that Asperger's syndrome potentially brings to your relationship, not all negative behaviors are due to AS. AS wiring may make your partner more susceptible to certain reactions and can also trigger serious reactions on your part. If either you or your partner loses patience with the other to such an extent that either of you demonstrates any of the following behaviors, there may be other serious issues that need attention. In that case, you may both benefit from seeking help from a professional counselor or psychotherapist.

* Hurtful verbal attacks

* Hitting or pushing

* Self-destructive behavior (such as excessive drinking, gambling, spending)

* Abuse of any kind

Asperger's syndrome does not offer you or your partner reasons to mistreat each other. These behaviors, on the part of either partner, can lead to serious consequences and should not be tolerated.

Points to Keep in Mind

Many behaviors related to Asperger's syndrome can make intimacy with an AS partner challenging. It may be hard to understand how your partner continually has no clue about the damage certain behaviors cause and how she can see things only from her own point of view. You might even start to wonder if your partner acts this way intentionally, although usually, no malicious intent exists. Your partner may need predictability and an increased understanding of social rules. Relationships can be exhausting when you are working hard to translate confusing social rules and nonverbal behavior.

Sometimes things seem worse before they get better; your hopes may be temporarily dashed. At this moment, your relationship may not feel quite healthy or fulfilling. You may grieve for your lost relationship dreams, as you realize that your partner may not be able to meet some of your needs and desires.

The future is full of possibilities. Before you knew you were dealing with Asperger's syndrome, there was no way to improve the situation. Now you know. To get and give the love you desire, you both have to change some of your current understanding and expectations. The end result can bring you and your partner to a deeper, more mature place in your love and commitment to one another.

CHAPTER 3

Embracing Differences

Our greatest strength as a human race is our ability to acknowledge our differences; our greatest weakness is our failure to embrace them.

—Judith Henderson

It may not be easy to accept that you and your partner are differently wired. We've looked at ways in which social interaction and behavior translate into relationship difficulties. In this chapter we delve deeper into understanding some of the natural differences between you and your partner. We also begin to explore ways of embracing them.

Empathizing and Systemizing

We can look at differences between you and your partner with Asperger's syndrome by considering differences in your respective abilities to empathize and systemize. *Empathy* involves identifying with and understanding another person's feelings or predicament. Empathizing often represents a general area of weakness for people with AS. *Systemizing* involves explaining, exploring, and creating groups whose members are related in various ways. People with AS often excel at understanding and analyzing systems.

Measuring the Differences

Simon Baron-Cohen, a psychologist well known for his research in autism, explored empathizing and systemizing in many people. He developed the Empathy Quotient (EQ) (Baron-Cohen and Wheelwright 2004) and the Systemizing Quotient (SQ) (Baron-Cohen et al. 2003), based on two questionnaires that uncover differences in thinking in these two areas. In general, non-AS women score higher in empathy than non-AS men, and non-AS men score higher in systemizing than non-AS women. Males and females with high-functioning autism and Asperger's tend to score lower in empathy and higher in systemizing than both non-AS females and non-AS males. These results offer one window into some of the differences in thinking and feeling between neurotypical people and people with Asperger's syndrome.

EXERCISE 3.1   The Empathy Quiz

This quiz has been adapted from Simon Baron-Cohen's EQ with permission. These statements about empathy will give you an idea of the kinds of differences you may see in how you and your partner relate to each other and people around you. If your partner takes the quiz and the result is a low rating, this doesn't show a lack of concern for others, only that he experiences and expresses concern differently.

Number a separate sheet of paper from 1 to 20 and respond to each statement, using the following scale:

Strongly agree	Slightly agree	Slightly disagree	Strongly disagree
a	b	c	d

If your partner also completes this quiz, that would be helpful and can be a starting point for discussion. If your partner doesn't take the empathy quiz, respond to the statements for yourself alone, and then respond again in the way that you think your partner would. No matter who responds to the statements, there's no right or wrong response, only the honest response.

1. I can easily tell if someone else wants to enter a conversation.

2. I find it difficult to explain to others things that I understand easily, when they don't understand them the first time.

3. People often tell me that I went too far in driving my point home in a discussion.

4. I often find it difficult to judge whether something is rude or polite.

5. In a conversation, I tend to focus on my own thoughts rather than what my listener might be thinking.

6. I can pick up on it quickly when someone says one thing but means another.

7. It is hard for me to see why some things upset people so much.

8. I find it easy to put myself in somebody else's shoes.

9. I am good at predicting how someone will feel.

10. I am quick to spot when someone in a group is feeling awkward or uncomfortable.

11. If I say something that inadvertently offends someone, I think it's that person's problem, not mine.

12. If someone asks me whether I like her haircut, I reply truthfully, even if I don't like it.

13. I can't always see why someone felt offended by a remark.

14. Other people tell me I am good at understanding how they are feeling and what they are thinking.

15. When I talk to people, I tend to talk about their experiences rather than my own.

16. It upsets me to see animals in pain.

17. I can make decisions without being influenced by people's feelings.

18. I get upset if I see people suffering on the TV news.

19. I can sense whether I am intruding, even if the other person doesn't tell me.

20. Other people often say that I am insensitive, though I don't always see why.

Your rating and what it means. After you have rated each of the twenty statements using the *a*-to-*d* scale, review your responses. Write 2 next to any *a* rating (strongly agree) and 1 next to any *b* rating (slightly agree) for statements 1, 6, 8, 9, 10, 14, 15, 16, 18, and 19. If you rated any of these statements as *c* or *d*, do not assign any numerical value.

Next, review your ratings for statements 2, 3, 4, 5, 7, 11, 12, 13, 17, and 20. For these statements, beside each rating of *c* (slightly disagree), write 1; and for each statement you gave a rating of *d* (strongly disagree), write 2. If you rated any of these statements as *a* or *b*, do not assign any numerical value.

Add up your points for a maximum total rating of 40. Your total is estimated based on my adaptation of the original Empathy Quotient, which has a maximum possible rating of 80 and is scientifically valid. This shorter version contains sample items, and scientific validity has not been established for this type of use.

Comparing your results with those of the original study, we can only approximate that a rating of 32 or over may suggest an extremely high capacity for empathy. A low empathy rating may be reflected in one that falls below 10. If this estimation doesn't seem to fit or if you want to check out the full version of the EQ, you can access the original journal article referenced in the back of this book (Baron-Cohen and Wheelwright 2004) or visit www .autismresearchcentre.com for the most updated sample of the test. You can also find a printed version of the EQ, the SQ, and two other tests at the back of Baron-Cohen's book *The Essential Difference* (2003).

For our purposes, reviewing your (and your partner's) responses to these statements about empathy will most likely expose a pattern regarding the way you each feel and express empathy and understanding. If your partner does not have an official AS diagnosis, a low empathy score does not mean she will be diagnosed with Asperger's. These two quizzes are not for diagnostic purposes but can help you to understand certain aspects of your relationship with your partner. Now take an informal, adapted version of Baron-Cohen's SQ and compare the two different patterns that may emerge.

EXERCISE 3.2   The Systemizing Quiz

Systemizing includes the attempt to understand rules and construct new systems. Number a separate sheet of paper from 1 to 20 and respond to the following twenty statements once for yourself and once in the way you think your partner would respond (unless your partner will answer for himself). Use the same rating system as for the EQ:

Strongly agree	Slightly agree	Slightly disagree	Strongly disagree
a	b	c	d

1. I find it difficult to read maps and understand them.

2. When I learn a language, I become intrigued by its grammatical rules.

3. If I had a collection (such as CDs, coins, or stamps), it would be highly organized.

4. I find it difficult to understand instruction manuals for putting appliances together.

5. When I look at a building, I am curious about the precise way it was constructed.

6. When traveling by train, I often wonder exactly how the rail networks are coordinated.

7. When I learn about historical events, I do not focus on exact dates.

8. I find it easy to grasp exactly how odds work in betting.

9. I do not enjoy games that involve a high degree of strategy (such as chess, Risk, Games Workshop).

10. When I look at an animal, I like to know the precise species it belongs to.

11. I am fascinated by how machines work.

12. I do not tend to watch science documentaries on television or read articles about science and nature.

13. When I look at a painting, I do not usually think about the technique involved in creating it.

14. I rarely read articles or web pages about new technology.

15. If I were buying a computer, I would want to know the exact details about its hard drive capacity and processor speed.

16. I do not read legal documents very carefully.

17. I am not very meticulous when I take on DIY projects or home improvements.

18. When I read the newspaper, I am drawn to tables of information, such as football league scores or the stock market index.

19. When I cook, I do not think about exactly how different methods and ingredients contribute to the final product.

20. When I listen to a piece of music, I always notice the way it's structured.

Your rating and what it means: After you have rated each of the twenty statements on the a-to-d scale, review your responses. Write 2 next to any a rating (strongly agree) and 1 next to any b rating (slightly agree) for statements 2, 3, 5, 6, 8, 10, 11, 15, 18, and 20. If you rated any of these statements as c or d, do not assign any numerical value.

Next, review your ratings for statements 1, 4, 7, 9, 12, 13, 14, 16, 17, and 19. For these statements, beside each rating of c (slightly disagree), write 1, and for each statement you gave a rating of d (strongly disagree), write 2. If you rated any of these statements as a or b, do not assign any numerical value.

Add up your points to get your total rating; the maximum number of possible points is, again, 40. Similar to the EQ, the original Systemizing Quotient had sixty questions, with a maximum rating of 80, and, unlike this shortened version, was scientifically valid.

Based on this adaptation of the original SQ, a total of at least 32 may only suggest that you have a very high systemizing rating, and ratings below 10 may suggest a very low systemizing rating. If you are interested in exploring the SQ further, you can review the original journal article (Baron-Cohen et al. 2003) or visit www.autismresearchcentre.com, where you can find a revised version of the SQ with new questions, plus many other informative surveys and questionnaires that may interest you.

Regardless of your exact rating, your responses to these statements highlight strengths and weaknesses, and help you to work on your relationship, where these differences can become paramount. The main thing to take away is not that either you or your partner lacks empathy or systemizing skills, but that the two of you have very different ways of thinking about the world.

Having a lower rating in systemizing than your partner doesn't mean that you don't have the capacity to learn how subway networks are coordinated or how architects design buildings. It probably does mean that you do not automatically seek that sort of knowledge or understand it as "common sense." Similarly, if your partner had a lower rating on the empathy quiz, it doesn't mean that she can't learn to increase understanding and appreciation of others' emotions, only that it might not come naturally to her.

Applying What You've Learned

If you and your partner are typical of couples in which one partner has Asperger's syndrome, you had a higher rating on the EQ, while your partner had a higher rating on the SQ. You may have responded that you find it easy to put yourself in somebody else's shoes, to do things at the spur of the moment, and to predict how others feel. Meanwhile, your partner with AS may feel that if he does something that offends someone, it's that person's problem, not his. Your partner may find it easy to understand instruction manuals for putting appliances together, while you can barely manage a bookshelf from IKEA. Your partner may focus on exact dates of historical events, while you can barely remember the events, let alone the date they occurred.

Empathy and Relationship Logic

Your ability to empathize with your partner helps you to figure out how to relate to her in various situations. People with Asperger's syndrome often have difficulty understanding such expectations. For example, Scott was not feeling well and wanted to go to bed earlier than usual to feel rested for work the next day. His partner with AS argued that this was not their usual bedtime and they would miss watching one of their favorite TV shows together. His partner's reaction in this situation left Scott feeling that his needs didn't matter to her. He could understand her disappointment in his changing their routine, but why was his perspective so unclear to her?

Due to Asperger's syndrome, your partner may not easily see your perspective, but can learn to accommodate you with a little help. In another couple, Joni wanted her partner to acknowledge that he hurt her by going into the bedroom to be alone and ignoring everyone at her party. Her point of view makes common sense socially to a neurotypical person. But for someone with Asperger's, the logic may not connect in the same way. Her partner, Carl, did not realize the importance of staying in the room during the party.

Carl experiences great discomfort at social gatherings from trying to handle the overwhelming noise and struggles of socializing with so many people at once. He logically believes that being in a comfortable setting holds greater importance than being overwhelmed at a party, regardless of what others think about that. I suggested that Carl take a break whenever he felt overwhelmed and come back to the party when he could. Then with some understanding, he made more of an effort in social situations, knowing how important it was to Joni for him to be there. Joni also allowed for the "break time," knowing that Carl was doing his best and would return when he felt he could.

With greater awareness of your partner's tendencies and the key differences between you, it becomes possible to bridge the gap between your different ways of being. Recognizing and appreciating your different needs and ways of expressing yourselves is crucial.

Your Relationship System

Relationships can be considered systems: they include rules for belonging and are made up of interrelated elements (you and your partner). Together, you have regular interactions and depend on each other in certain ways. Your relationship interactions create some predictable patterns and boundaries. You two, as a couple, are different from you two as individuals. Your relationship is an entity unto itself, a system.

Like any system, your relationship includes unwritten rules for both you and your partner about how you should act (the hidden curriculum). Non-AS partners often take the relationship "system" for granted, because understanding the many unwritten rules and expectations comes naturally for them. Partners with AS typically have difficulty analyzing the relationship system. Unlike other systems, such as the system of electrical wiring or the system of trains in your town, rules and behavior in relationships can be unpredictable and hard to decode.

People often do not follow predictable patterns. For example, you may react differently in similar situations depending on your mood or other factors. Apparently, a desire for predictability in successful intimate relationships is not just an AS issue. Ellen Fein and Sherrie Schneider's dating book, *The Rules* (1995), was a number one *New York Times* best seller. But it may be more difficult for someone with Asperger's syndrome to be flexible with rules, or to go with the flow when a rule has an exception or does not work at all in certain situations.

Bridging the Gap

In some ways, your varied strengths and weaknesses can make you and your partner a great match. Your differences can, at times, complement each other and help you, as a couple, to be very successful in many areas. At other times, your differences may not work in such a complementary way. If people see your partner as insensitive and your partner cannot see why—when she insists that it is your problem that her behavior offended you, not hers, when she is so meticulous about putting your appliances together that you wait over a month for her to finish with the washing machine—things can begin to feel less than complementary.

All of these areas can improve with patience and persistence. For example, your AS partner can learn to understand why you and others interpret his behavior as offensive and insensitive. This chapter and several future chapters, most notably chapter 7, on communication, cover working with disagreements and necessary compromises that may arise as a result of some of your basic differences.

Using Systems in Your Relationship

The more you can translate your relationship system into predictable patterns or explicit rules, the more your partner may be able to be a positive participant. It may be difficult for you to think concretely and formally, but using systems in your relationship can be invaluable for helping your partner with organization, decision making, and household management. For example, organization checklists and flowcharts provide visual aids that systematize various chores and responsibilities. These tools can help your partner understand exactly what you want and successfully fulfill your expectations. Making the rules explicit in your relationship is also important, and chapter 8 includes activities to help you do so.

The following are a few examples of systems that you can begin implementing today to help your relationship system run more smoothly. Start with the ones that seem most helpful and relevant for you and your partner. You should see results in a short time, which will hopefully help to motivate you to continue working with your partner in this way or to be creative in finding ways that are more helpful for your situation.

ORGANIZATION

You may need to experiment with various organizational methods to find the ones that work best for you and your partner. Look for ways to help you work together as a team. Many people with Asperger's syndrome seem better at understanding visual information (what they see) than auditory information (what they hear). Therefore, information sometimes proves most helpful when it comes in the form of visual aids, such as pictures, lists, and charts. Organizational systems work best when you and your partner work together to develop them.

* *Checklists* can be useful for increasing productivity throughout the day. You can have a list of chores, a shopping list, a list of errands, and so on.

* *Calendars and planners* can help coordinate personal and relationship activities. Remind your partner to check your shared calendar and add dates both in her personal planner

and on the calendar. Update the calendar together regularly.

*   *Establish a schedule* together that outlines when important tasks will be done and by whom. For example, you can agree to put aside an hour per week for paying bills or a morning per week for cleaning.

*   *Organize items* needed to complete a given task; for example, use a drawer to contain the checkbook, pen, calculator, and receipts. Or store a bucket filled with cleaning supplies in the bathroom closet.

*   *Chore charts* serve as a common visual aid used by couples for household organization and management. Instead of a household chore chart, you can also use a checklist of daily or weekly tasks.

In the following sample chart, each partner initials the appropriate box when he or she completes that particular chore. Sometimes it works best when you preplan who does what and when. For some couples, it works to simply agree on how many of the boxes should end up with each of your initials and let it go from there. Including yourself on the chart and even doing chores together can help get things done.

TABLE 3.1   Sample Chore Chart

Daily Chores	Mon	Tue	Wed	Thur	Fri	Sat	Sun
Make bed.							
Feed pets.							
Take dishes to sink / help clear table.							
Wash dishes or fill dishwasher.							
Check kitchen trash; take out if full.							

Twice-Weekly Chores								
Mop kitchen floor.								
Clean litter box.								
Weekly Chores								
Wash and dry clothes; fold and put away.								
Take trash out every Tuesday.								
Shop for food.								
Vacuum living room.								

This chart is just one example; there are many ways to make one, and you can find other examples in books and online. In general, several lists or charts work better than one big, confusing one. For instance, you can have one chart just for yard work (collecting trash, raking leaves, weeding, watering, mowing, edging, and cleaning up), one for household chores, and one for household projects.

Try not to get bogged down in the particulars of this specific chart. People hold different standards, and you probably maintain different standards than your partner does. For example, some people change their bedsheets every few days; some change them once a month or less frequently.

You need to decide with your partner how often certain chores should get done, such as washing the car, cleaning the refrigerator, vacuuming, or changing sheets. This may take a bit of negotiation. For instance, if you want the kitchen floor mopped daily and your partner thinks it needs to be done only a couple of times a month, maybe you can agree to his mopping it two or three times per month and your mopping the rest of the time for now. Your partner may later be more cooperative about doing a chore because you see it as necessary, as the teamwork aspect of your relationship grows.

Sometimes you can agree to one another's standards or negotiate a trade. Your partner might dust every day if you keep your shoes in the closet, not all over the bedroom floor. Such negotiation or compromises are a hidden-curriculum concept that may need direct instruction for someone with AS. If you cannot agree on household management issues, a counselor can help you and your partner to negotiate these tasks and come up with a plan.

Work together to decide how much or how little detail you need to get a job done. If you want your partner to do something with many steps, you may need to provide those steps, for example, steps for cleaning the bathroom, kitchen, or bedroom. Something simple for you, such as watering the plants, may also need specific instructions. One of you may feel that certain tasks need to be performed in a certain way. When a compromise can't be reached, the person who cares the most about how a specific task gets done can become responsible for that task. You either have to teach each other how you expect the task to be done, let the other partner handle it, or lower your standards when possible and accept the way your partner completes the job.

Reward yourselves for a job well done. Once you check off your entire list for the day, take at least one-half to one hour to do something for yourself, such as talk on the phone, read a chapter of a book, or take a bath. Help your partner do the same. For example, once your partner checks her list off each day, encourage her to take an hour of totally quiet time or computer time, or time to lie in bed and do nothing—guilt free.

DECISION MAKING AND PROBLEM SOLVING

Decision making includes working as a team to support each other's goals or the goals of your household, such as handling money, dealing with your children, or deciding where to go on vacation. It can be difficult to deal with your partner's sometimes-frustrating, circular thinking, based on literal Aspergian logic. One partner with AS, Alex, spends a good deal of time with a coworker named Casey. Devyn, Alex's partner, expressed concerns about this relationship, but Alex insisted, "Nothing illicit is going on." While truthfully, no inappropriate physical contact took place, it was not clear that nothing was going on. Devyn continued to feel threatened, but Alex was unable to see or consider Devyn's point of view until we discussed it and appealed to his logical understanding. Alex finally understood the importance of considering Devyn's uncomfortable feelings about the situation and agreed to spend less time with

Casey. This agreement took a while, as Alex's rationalizations led us around in circles until we put a new problem-solving system into play.

Have a system for decision making. This can help your partner participate with you in making decisions without leaving both of you going around in circles. As an example, try the following model of decision making the next time there's a decision you need to make with your partner.

1. State the problem or decision to be made. In this example, the problem for Devyn is that Alex spends too much time with Casey.

2. Have a brainstorming session around solutions. Sometimes only two solutions require consideration: making the decision or not. Sometimes other possibilities need exploration. In this example, Alex could completely stop spending time with Casey, continue spending lots of time together, or spend time with Casey but less of it.

3. Evaluate your solutions. Discuss the pros and cons of each possibility. This system undoubtedly works the best with input from both of you. In this case, Alex first insisted that nothing change. Devyn insisted that Alex and Casey should not spend so much time together.

4. Make a decision. Both partners agreed that Alex would eat lunch with Casey only once a week, unless the whole group ate lunch together.

5. Follow through and then reevaluate to make sure this solution works. If not, redo the process and try another solution that might work. In this case, both partners felt okay with this decision three months later. In fact, Alex made new friends at work, and Devyn no longer feels threatened. If this decision proved unsatisfactory to either one of them for any reason, we would redo the process to find where further agreement could be reached.

Visual aids can help the decision-making process. A flowchart clarifies decisions and possible consequences, making them easier to understand. Information presented in a step-by-step diagram can help your AS partner to focus and be an active contributor at each step, without feeling overwhelmed by the big picture.

Flowcharts can reach a point of hindering rather than helping with decisions, if you or your partner gets bogged down in the act of detailing the chart with fancy symbols and elaborate actions. For both of you to use it easily, keep the flowchart as simple and narrowly focused as possible. It works better to use several flowcharts to detail different decisions or problems than a big, elaborate one that meanders around the page with different consequences, outcomes, and new decisions to be made. This can become an organizational nightmare and end up being more confusing than helpful.

Making a flowchart begins with determining what decision you need to make. Draw a small square or rectangle either toward the left of a large piece of paper or in the middle of the top. Inside the shape, write down the decision you need to make. Use arrows or lines to connect other shapes that represent possible solutions and consequences of your potential decisions, showing the flow of the process. Two examples of simple flowcharts follow.

Figure 3.1 Sample Flowchart A

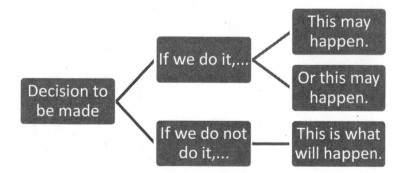

A flowchart filled with a decision to be made looks like this.

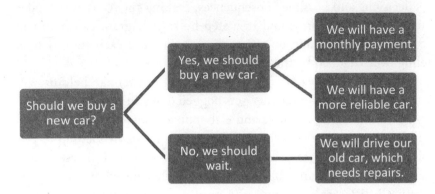

As you can see, sometimes the flow leads to another decision to be made. You and your partner might need to work out your budget to see if you can handle a new monthly payment. You can spell this out in a new flowchart or, if it involves only another step or two, extend this chart farther to the right. Remember not to make it too complicated.

The next flowchart is similar to the previous one but works in a top-down direction rather than left to right. Choose the one that works best for you and your partner.

Figure 3.2 Sample Flowchart B

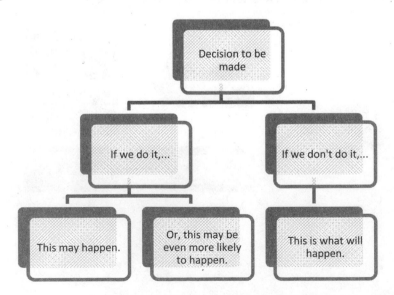

Be flexible and creative in your methods. If, for example, your partner wants things to remain the same and struggles to make any changes, try focusing on the consequences of waiting. Make a list of pros and cons, outlining all of the logical reasons you can think of in your rationale for buying a new car. Putting your budget in writing might help with your logical argument; a new car may be both necessary and affordable.

Sometimes, even after trying everything you can, you can't reach a mutual decision. As for one couple I know, the AS partner becomes so anxious about any kind of change that her partner feels that he must make big decisions unilaterally or they won't get made. One way he dealt with this particular situation was by going out on his own and buying a new car. This method is not recommended, but life does go on for this couple, and except for such moments, they continue living very happily together.

You may not need or want increased structure, but your partner may need it to help with time management, organization, and direction. You can reduce your own and your partner's stress by addressing decisions to be made or tasks and responsibilities that need to get done in a less-overwhelming way. If you currently take on too much responsibility, spending time and energy now to put organizational systems in place will be worth the effort and end up freeing you rather than limiting you further.

Points to Keep in Mind

There are many ways to bridge the gap between the empathic and systems-oriented ways of being that may come between you and your partner. Logical systems of action can sound too scientific to you, but might help you get more of what you need in your relationship. In an Internet thread I read recently, someone complained that her AS partner didn't share in the workload at home. She wished she had a system for getting things done. This elicited a response from a blogger with AS, who suggested this couple try the System of Scientific Management, developed in 1911 by Frederick W. Taylor.

Using this scientific system to complete household chores might improve efficiency but would probably leave a non-AS partner feeling very unhappy. Taylor's system may be too extreme for home use, but developing a rational plan of action can be just the thing to help get things done around the house. Simple chore lists, such as the one described, come closer to a compromise between no structure for getting chores done and a "scientific" method.

Much of the rest of this book is dedicated to increasing your connection to your partner so that you both feel loved and satisfied in your relationship. Emotional give-and-take may come easier for you than for your more practical-minded partner with Asperger's syndrome. You have to be careful about what you give and take, though. The neurotypical way is not the only or even best way. As you listen to your partner, you can grow in understanding the logic and practicality of life and love.

CHAPTER 4

The Heart of Your Relationship

*Love at first sight is easy to understand; it's when two people have
been looking at each other for a lifetime that it becomes a miracle.*

—Sam Levenson

Is love blind? Or is there more to it? The way your relationship evolved
contains lessons for its continuing growth. The love that develops based
on overwhelming, positive feelings carries us through when we begin to
enter more realistic phases of the relationship. Over time you begin to
see your partner more clearly and slowly start seeing her faults. Often,
with commitment and effort, the pendulum swings back into a balance
of mature love. At this point in your relationship, you may be focused
primarily on faults. But chances are that your relationship did not start
out this way.

Yours may not be a fairy-tale relationship, but it had a "once upon a time" and can potentially have a "happily ever after." We may have to redefine "happily ever after," but that comes later. We first start at the beginning, the part where you two found each other and began to feel some sort of attraction. Understanding the beginning of your relationship with your AS partner may help you to rekindle excitement and warm feelings. It is also important to look back at your initial attraction to understand how you came to partner with someone who has AS; your relationship development was most likely not one sided.

For many reasons, both conscious and unconscious, you chose your partner. Often the non-AS partner initiates the relationship, because the partner with AS may not realize your interest until you make a move that makes it very clear. Understanding your own internal hopes, motivations, and other reasons for choosing your current partner often helps to focus the growth of the relationship differently.

Your partner's behavior may play an important role for you; many partners I meet have had more than one relationship with someone with AS, and this is probably not a coincidence. If you find yourself developing relationships with a number of people with similar characteristics, there is probably an important reason within you. Your partner most likely met some very important needs (and hopefully still does) and may actually be a good match for you.

This chapter helps you explore your partnership in more depth as you make a deeper commitment to put more energy into making your relationship work. Remembering your love story can help to remind you of the good things about your relationship that still remain. Revisiting the beginning of your relationship and viewing your current differences in a more positive light can strengthen your intimate partnership.

Some of the ways in which your partner initially interacted with you probably entered into your attraction to him. For one thing, he may have been especially attentive in the beginning. This often holds true in developing relationships, although with Asperger's syndrome, attentiveness can be intensified by the AS partner's tendency toward a strong, single-minded focus. Your partner may be overattentive because he wants to learn everything he can about you.

When you first get to know your partner, the symptoms of Asperger's can be subtle and hard to recognize. Your partner may have many attributes that come across very well. Therefore it often takes time for partners like you to realize that your relationship interactions seem different from interactions between two neurotypical partners.

At times, the very behaviors and attitudes we found initially attractive in our partners can eventually turn us off. In the beginning of your relationship, your partner's knowledge of history and all of the amazing facts he remembers and recites may seem fascinating. Perhaps you fell in love with his strong, silent presence. Later, you may feel bored at hearing about the Civil War at every social event, or wish he expressed more of his feelings. Your charming, brilliant, and engaging partner can now seem rude and cold, or, at best, naive.

Falling in Love

What attracts people to each other varies, as does what carries us through when things go awry. For neurotypical partners, falling in love may be based more on emotions than for the more practical and logical-minded people with Asperger's syndrome. When you think about your partner, do you focus on how he makes you *feel* or what you *think* about him? Non-AS partners typically focus more on feelings, while partners with AS tend to think more practically and rationally about relationships.

Attraction Based on Emotion

Men and women with AS are often physically attractive, brilliant, well educated, and successful in their careers. The apparently strong, quiet men with Asperger's seem to offer kindness and attentiveness. Such men typically attract partners who prefer a sensitive and intellectual man. The typical guy with AS does not come across as macho; although his partner may feel abandoned at times, the usual culprits are not likely to be sports, beer, or other women. Women with AS can appear strong and independent. These women may be attractive to partners who view them as "low maintenance," or not as emotionally demanding as other women.

When you first met your partner, you were likely charmed by intelligence and sincerity. She may have been very attentive and dependable, with a strong sense of moral and ethical justice. These qualities, along with other AS advantages, provide a strong foundation for emotion-based attraction. But the main way that neurotypical partners seem to think about falling in love has to do with the way a love interest makes them feel and how they feel about her.

Tony Attwood, a psychologist practicing in Australia who is well known for his work in the field of autism and Asperger's syndrome, observes that partners of people on the autism spectrum often fall on the opposite end of the empathy continuum from their autistic partners. Attwood refers to the neurotypical partners as "intuitive experts" because they show a very good understanding of, and empathy toward, the perspectives of others (Attwood 2007b). People with Asperger's may be competent in their careers or special-interest topics, yet vulnerable and naive in social situations. Many people who love someone with AS provide their partners with understanding and compassion along with social guidance. Your strengths here may help your partner to grow and develop in the social and emotional areas of relating.

Attraction Based on Practical Issues and Logic

People with Asperger's syndrome sometimes recognize their need for someone who is good at socializing, and therefore seek a partner who can be their "better half." They may be attracted to neurotypical partners for the way the potential partner can make up for their own social difficulties. Someone with AS may look for a partner with similar interests yet with enough differences to help compensate for personal weaknesses.

Attwood suggests that males with AS more often develop relationships with non-AS partners, while females with AS more often couple with a partner who also has AS (Attwood 2007a). Men with AS tend to seek someone who can compensate for their areas of social and organizational weakness, and select a partner at the opposite end of the empathy scale (Baron-Cohen 2003). Women with AS more often tend to select a partner with more similarities in terms of expectations and lifestyle choices (Attwood 2007a).

Either way, people with AS appear less likely to describe a love based on how they feel. Rather, they may describe falling in love based on the way they believe they fit together with a partner or the way they think about a partner's wonderful and special attributes. Your partner likely feels good being around you and feels love for you, or he would not choose to be with you; but he is less likely to describe attraction in those terms. His strengths may be more about developing the "space in your togetherness" suggested by philosopher Kahlil Gibran (1972, 15), which is so important for personal growth and independence.

The Influence of Past Relationships

You've heard that history repeats itself, and this applies to relationship history as well. Your first and most significant relationships occur in your family of origin, and these relationships can affect all future relationships one way or another. If you look closely at your relationship, you will probably find some patterns that have been repeated from your past, or if not repeated, avoided. Past experiences helped to shape you and your relationship. When you become aware of past influence, you can make more conscious choices and minimize any negative impact of your past on you and your relationship.

EARLY FAMILY RELATIONSHIPS

Your past history of relationships can contribute to your attraction to someone with Asperger's syndrome. Certain patterns in your current relationship with your AS partner may share similar traits with relationships in your family of origin, or may express opposite traits. You may be attracted to a strong woman with AS because your own mother seemed weak and dependent. If your father exhibited a lot of macho behavior, you may find yourself attracted to the gentleness of a man with AS. If one of your parents had Asperger's or was emotionally unavailable to you in some way, you may be attracted to a partner who is also unavailable emotionally. Early family relationships may be affecting your experiences in your current relationship.

Our families of origin provide the first and most important model for what to expect in relationships. You may not consciously like certain behavior, but it may be associated with love based on how the important people who loved you treated you. You may wish for something different, but on a deep level, certain behaviors that came to be associated with love might feel "normal." When you explore your unconscious reasons for choosing your partner, you can stay and work it through or consciously choose another partner. In moving toward a more emotionally gratifying relationship, it helps to challenge your assumptions and develop new expectations for yourself and your partnership.

Relationships grow in different ways. Taking a look at how yours developed provides insight into why you fell for your partner and highlights relationship strengths that can be tapped to make positive changes. Sometimes "love at first sight" sparks instantaneously when two people first meet, and they each "know" they have met the person they want to spend their lives with. Other times, a couple may feel some chemistry but need to take more time to get to know one another better before embarking on a long-term relationship. Regardless of the way people meet, past relationships often influence attitudes and behavior in current relationships.

Love at First Sight

Falling in love immediately on meeting another, love at first sight, usually stems from either a strong physical attraction or a phenomenon known in the psychology world as *projection*. Lots of long-term relationships start out in one of these ways, often motivated by unconscious desires, such as finding a partner who treats you as someone in your childhood did.

Physical attraction represents an important feature in choosing a partner. Most people want to be at least somewhat physically attracted to a potential partner. Physical attraction can grow in either direction as you gain deeper knowledge of another person. One woman married to a man with Asperger's told me that for her current marriage, which was her third, she purposely went for good looks because, as she put it, "at least when we argue, I have some motivation to try to love him again."

Projection happens when we believe we know what others think or feel based on our own experiences. When we project thoughts or beliefs onto someone else, our information (our thoughts) about that person may have nothing at all to do with her. Sometimes our assumptions prove correct, sometimes wrong. Regardless, our guesswork feels like fact. Different people can view a quiet person with AS, for example, as intellectual, dull, shy, arrogant, attentive, inattentive, a good listener, cold, thoughtful, uncaring, and so on—same person, different projections by others.

During the lustful stage of a strong physical attraction, or the projection stage, when we think we know our partner, couples sometimes quickly feel the love and move in together. In these situations, couples sometimes fall in love with who they think the other person is, not who that person really is. This is a common complaint of partners who end up in a relationship with someone who has AS. Perhaps you hold beliefs and expectations of your partner based on what you hoped or thought he had to offer, not on actual evidence. In this case, you must now go back to your assumptions, which hold your hopes and dreams, and try to reconcile them realistically with your current relationship reality. I will help you do this throughout this book.

If you or your partner chose each other based on lust that has since fizzled or on personal misperceptions, you can take heart in knowing that a more mature love can still grow if you both want to be together. You may have missed important information about your partner's AS in the beginning of your relationship, but many couples move through this phase and develop a deep connection. Now that you are gaining a deeper understanding of your partner, you can still love her, even though you may have to change your expectations and unrealistic ideas about her. There may be initial disappointment, but through your love, you can adjust your expectations and love your partner for her true self.

EXERCISE 4.1   Why Did You Fall in Love?

Now it's time to get back to the heart of your relationship and consider the characteristics that attracted you to your partner, what they mean in your relationship today, and what changes you may need to make. The sample exercise, "Why I Fell in Love," provides an example of how to complete this exercise. It combines initial reasons for choosing your partner with important initial thoughts or feelings about your relationship and changes you would now like to see.

1. Make three columns with the following headings: "Initial attraction," "What I thought or felt," and "Is it still working?"

2. In the first column, write down the characteristics that initially attracted you to your partner. Consider the attributes that attracted you and why they felt so much like love. Was it something about your partner's looks, smile, or mannerisms? Think about situations you enjoyed and lovable characteristics your partner possesses.

3. Take time to reflect on why these particular aspects of a partner were important to you. In the second column, write any relevant thoughts that come to mind. Consider what needs you were looking for that your partner met for you.

4. Now think about your current feelings in your relationship. In the third column, write about whether the initial aspects of attraction still work for you or whether you need to make changes. In the next chapter, I will help you develop goals to get started on making these changes.

5. Have your partner complete this exercise, and talk about it together. Knowledge of what your partner found attractive in you may help you to further your understanding about how you came to be in your current relationship and what some of his underlying expectations may be. Such understanding can help you to go beyond dissatisfaction and resentment to a deeper connection with your partner.

This exploration, even if your partner chooses not to participate, will help you in your own work toward a conscious, more fulfilling relationship. With or without your partner's answers, it helps to remember "the good old days," which form the foundation, or heart, of your partnership. Your responses help to clarify your initial choice and help you to better understand how you came to be partnered with someone who possesses both the strengths and challenges of Asperger's syndrome.

SAMPLE EXERCISE 4.1 Why I Fell in Love

Initial attraction	What I thought or felt	Is it still working?
Love at first sight. We clicked right away.	I thought I knew everything he was thinking; he reminded me of my favorite cousin.	We still click in many ways but need more intimate talks, which are difficult for him.
Physical attraction: he is tall, dark, and handsome.	Anybody would want someone who looks like that.	With someone so good looking attracted to me, I overlooked a lot that we need to look at now.
Shared interests: we worked together on the library archives and have a similar work ethic.	I loved talking about history and books with someone so brilliant. I thought I had found my soul mate.	I realize that it's his special interest; he never stops talking about it, which makes me not want to discuss it.
Specific personality traits: he is soft spoken, funny, and kind.	He is the opposite of most men in my life.	He is a kind and loyal gentleman; I love him for that.
Specific skills: he is handy around the house, good at investing, and fun with kids.	These traits were definitely on my wish list for an ideal partner.	He does a lot of good things that benefit our household and relationship.

Good Times

Remembering the good old days can help you to get in touch with positive hopes and feelings again. The way you chose your partner says something about you and how you ended up in your current relationship. It also holds part of the solution to gaining more happiness and satisfaction. While it helps to be aware of why you ended up in your current relationship, it is also important to remember that you can make it work anyway. Even couples in arranged marriages who did not choose each other or who initially had little in common have ended up in strong, loving relationships (Epstein 2010). You chose your partner, and regardless of the reasons, you can have a strong, loving relationship too.

EXERCISE 4.2   Writing Your Love Story

The purpose of this exercise is to revisit your initial romance and good feelings and the reasons you wanted to get together with your partner in the first place.

1. Take fifteen minutes now to write about how your relationship started and to remember the loving part of your relationship story. If you are not comfortable writing, you can find a quiet place to focus on your love story and explore the questions introspectively. Either way, do step 4 in writing to have some written reference to go back to. Later (in exercise 4.3), you will complete your love story.

2. Start your entry or your reflections with "Once upon a time..." and write in the third person. In other words, write as if your story were about someone else.

3. Answer the following questions: How did you meet? How did you first feel about your partner? Include at least three things you loved about your partner when you started dating.

4. End the story at a positive point. If you live together, end the story at the point at which you moved in. Otherwise, end it at a high point in your relationship. Do not end it with "and they lived happily ever after" or on a negative note.

Sometimes, by the time we truly get to know someone, we already live with that person and are deeply immersed in an intimate relationship. If we don't pay close attention, the relationship can evolve to a disappointing place. Perhaps the neurological differences between you and your partner have brought you to such a place. Remembering the initial more trouble-free and loving part of your relationship can help you to get in touch with how much you love your partner and why it's worth it to keep trying to make your relationship work.

When the Pendulum Swings

Maybe you are one of those naturally nurturing and empathic partners. You have really understood and been patient with your partner throughout the years, and perhaps feel little or no appreciation. Much of the maintenance of the relationship and day-to-day responsibilities may be yours alone. While you tend to understand your partner's needs and perspective, your partner may not naturally reciprocate. This, in a nutshell, may have eroded some of your positive feelings and clouded them with built-up resentment. Regardless of where your relationship stands right now, consider a future positive ending to your love story.

EXERCISE 4.3   Completing Your Love Story

Complete your love story the way you wish it to be. In the next chapter, you will use your dreams about your relationship to help you develop realistic relationship goals.

Write the last paragraph of your love story. What ideally happened after they (you and your partner) moved in together or as the relationship grew? If you could have anything happen in the relationship to have the characters (you and your partner) live happily ever after, what would that be?

A mature relationship need not lack love and romance. Both you and your partner had a role in your developing relationship, and you both have a role in improving it so that each of you feels happy and satisfied. Returning to the heart of the matter by remembering your love story can help to remind you of what brought you together and to highlight the characteristics of your relationship that can keep you in love.

Points to Keep in Mind

A host of personal qualities, needs, and desires form the basis of our attraction to potential partners. You may be overly caring and look for ways to offer your loving energy. You may have unconscious assumptions about your partner or relationships in general. You may still be responding to old parental messages or unfinished business. For these and other reasons, you find yourself in a relationship with someone who has Asperger's syndrome.

The initial courtship makes way for a more mature relationship. Some of what attracts you in the beginning can eventually make life with your partner more difficult. For instance, although you may have been attracted to your partner's quiet demeanor, it may now embarrass you that she does not speak much at parties. Similarly, her strong opinions may have once led to your admiration but now lead to contempt as she voices them at inappropriate times.

Understanding why you came to be in a relationship with someone with AS can also help balance some of the resentment and anger that may develop. The next chapter focuses on developing realistic goals to move your relationship toward the places you dreamed it would go.

CHAPTER 5

Meeting Your Needs

Love does not exist in gazing at each other, but in looking outward together in the same direction.

—Antoine de Saint-Exupéry

The ending of your love story sets the scene for meeting your needs. Working toward your ideals leads to increased happiness and satisfaction for both you and your partner. You may see your dreams as unrealistic, and for today they might be. But you can turn your dreams into long-term goals that can be broken down into smaller, specific steps to help you to slowly work toward your big goals: your relationship dreams.

This chapter focuses on helping you to understand your needs and develop goals to meet them. Change must move slowly for you and your partner with Asperger's syndrome. Decide which issues or needs feel most pressing, and give them the highest priority. Move down your list one item at a time, as each issue and your overall relationship improve.

What You Need and How to Get It

We all have needs. The needs of someone who has Asperger's syndrome and the needs of someone without it can be very different, sometimes even opposing. The following table presents a list of many common relationship needs. Although this table divides needs into three columns based on whether or not you have Asperger's, in reality, divisions are not entirely clear cut. Someone with AS can have any of the needs in column 1, such as the need for approval or passion, and someone without AS can have needs that are in the AS column, such as the need for a calm environment or for control. The needs in this table are sorted by the most common differences seen between partners with and without Asperger's syndrome, but everyone is unique and cannot be held to a strict stereotype.

TABLE 5.1   Common Relationship Needs

Common Non-AS Needs	Common Needs for Both	Common AS Needs
Adventure	Acknowledgment	A calm environment
Approval	Appreciation	Certainty
Being needed	Being heard	Consistency
Being noticed	Concern	Control
Commitment	Encouragement	Direct requests
Compliments	Feeling important	Information
Connection / intimacy	Honesty	Logical explanations
Excitement	Loving me as I am	Practicality
Going out	Loyalty	Predictability
More help with chores	Organization	Preparation
Passion	Protection	Punctuality
Reassurance	Respect	Quiet
Spontaneity	Safety	Routine
Surprises	Security	Solitude
Time together	Support	Specific instructions
Touching	Trust	Stability
Verbal affection	Understanding	Structure
Variety	Valued for accomplishments	Time for special interest

Some needs shown in this table may be nonnegotiable, such as your need for commitment and loyalty, or your partner's need for a certain amount of solitude and calm. Other needs may be open for compromise, such as your need for surprises or your partner's need for control. Needs that prove absolutely essential and needs that can be negotiated vary from person to person.

Identifying Needs

The first step in getting your needs met is to identify them so that you can know what they are and clearly ask for them to be met.

EXERCISE 5.1 Defining the Essentials

This exercise helps you to narrow down your needs so that you can work on getting them met in your relationship.

1. Write at least ten needs that apply to you in your current relationship. Look at all three lists in table 5.1 to find qualities that you believe would make you feel more loved by your partner. You can use words not found on those lists if they more adequately express your needs.

2. Compare each of your needs and identify your highest priorities. Rewrite your list in order of priority, with your most crucial needs at the top of the list.

You can do this exercise with your partner by, together, identifying at least five needs that you both share and branching out from there into the areas where your needs vary. Using this exercise to identify your partner's needs will also help you learn to reconcile your needs with his in order to keep you both feeling loved and cared for. If you must do this exercise alone, use what you know about your partner to take his needs into account. This valuable information will help you proceed to make important changes in your relationship.

Getting Your Needs Met

Each of us maintains responsibility for getting our own needs met. Your partner may not realize that she does not meet your needs. Similarly, you may believe that you meet her needs, but are you sure? Unmet needs often form the basis for criticism, impatience, and disagreements. Positive and direct conversations that focus on meeting the needs of both partners can be helpful when they happen regularly in your relationship.

HELPFUL STRATEGIES

Clearly and specifically asking your partner for what you want is an important step in getting it from him. Many non-AS partners assume their partners with Asperger's syndrome know what they need but withhold it. Why else does he watch you carry heavy bags or wait for you to handle dinner even when you feel sick? He may not intuit your needs.

Consider this request: "I'm going out for a few hours. Can you please do the yard work?" It might be obvious to you that in this context, "yard work" means bagging the leaves. After all, it is October, the leaves cover your yard, and you marked the leaf pickup on the calendar for this Friday. But without more specific information, your partner with AS could spend the afternoon pruning overgrown bushes. It might be more useful to say, "Can you please rake the leaves and put them in the leaf bags by the curb for Friday's pickup?" Specific and direct communication helps in many situations and prevents building resentment.

The point is to share your needs with your partner so that she can tell exactly what you want. She also needs to see the logic in why she should do it. For some things, making you happy will be enough of a reason. But not many of us agree to do absolutely whatever it takes in the service of pleasing someone, especially if the request seems to make no apparent sense.

Set aside time to talk with your partner about one of your concerns, or ask specifically for what you want, such as help with the grocery bags. Be as specific and straightforward as possible: "Can you please get the remaining bags from the trunk of the car and carry them into the kitchen?" versus "Why don't you get up and do something to help me?" The latter way of expressing your need is nonspecific. Your partner may get up and try to figure out the best way to help. Perhaps he will hold the door for you or pick up the cat so that she does not get outside. He may sincerely try to help and be taken aback by your anger.

Specificity is very important. Another common complaint includes this one from Nancy. She makes a fuss about her partner's birthday, and when hers rolls around, she expects something special. She feels disappointed every year on her birthday, because her partner never makes any special effort. When we spoke, Nancy told me that she was sure her partner could tell when she felt upset, because she would get very quiet at these times and avoid him for the night. "He knows what I want but doesn't follow through," she told me. Nancy resisted my suggestion to let her partner know where and when to make reservations, and exactly what she wanted to happen on her birthday at least one week before it came up. Recently, when she finally gave it a try, she celebrated the best birthday since her relationship began, seven years ago.

Maybe you've never specifically told your partner what you need, or maybe you've grown tired of telling her over and over again. Try it differently this time; use logic and try not to get overemotional. In getting your point across, be clear, sincere, and specific. Address your needs one at a time, gradually dealing with each one. This will remain necessary throughout the course of your relationship. Assuming that your partner already knows and understands what you need causes many misunderstandings.

The Importance of Goals

Once you define what you want and make this clear to yourself and your partner, more focused work may be necessary to get your needs met. Setting goals for this purpose helps you to discover where you want to go and to develop steps to move in that direction. A clear picture of where your ideas and visions differ from those of your partner, as well as where they come together, helps define your relationship and the work to be done. Sharing goals and dreams helps you to have a closer bond with your partner as you develop a shared vision of the future.

In developing goals, choosing where to begin may be difficult, but it is important to narrow your focus for now. You can always come back and work more on one goal, but you cannot work on everything at once. Any area you work on will begin to change the chemistry in your overall relationship and will affect more than just a single issue. Write as many goals as you can, prioritize them, and then start with a few of the easiest ones first. The exercises in this chapter show how to develop goals, but there are a couple of points to remember before you start.

Finding Middle Ground

When your partner has Asperger's syndrome, one of the most important relationship skills for working on goals lies in your ability to compromise. This takes a good deal of perseverance, negotiation, and creativity. The best relationship compromises involve both partners getting something their way. You belong to the same team, so if one of you loses, it means a loss for the team. A win involves both of you having your needs met, even if some needs get compromised for the good of your relationship. Finding win-win compromises may prove to be tough, especially with the difficulties that change and compromise pose in your relationship due to Asperger's syndrome. Compromising now will be worth the effort to develop a more satisfying partnership. If a win-win situation doesn't seem possible, the 1-to-10 scale can sometimes help in deciding the outcome.

TABLE 5.2   The 1-to-10 Scale

10	Utmost importance
9	Extremely important
8	Very important
7	Somewhat important
6	Slightly important
5	Important but open
4	Not that important
3	Care a little
2	Don't care
1	Couldn't care less

This concept is somewhat self-explanatory, and you can use it in various situations in your relationship. Basically if you and your partner disagree about something, you can each rate it on a scale of 1 to 10. A rating of 1 means that although you have an opinion about the matter, you really do not care if it goes another way. A rating of 10 means that this issue holds utmost importance for you. If you and your partner disagree, you can rate the ideas or the situation, and let the bigger "win" go to the partner to whom the issue seems most important.

REALITY C: YOUR RELATIONSHIP REALITY

In long-term intimate relationships, your reality (reality A) and your partner's reality (reality B) end up meshing into a new reality: reality C. Some partners of people with AS complain that they end up giving themselves up and taking on too many "Asperger ways" after living too long with an AS partner. On the other hand, people with AS often end up feeling as if everything they do must meet neurotypical standards. The nature of Asperger's does make it difficult for your partner to compromise at times, and sometimes you may bend farther in trying to avoid his anger or withdrawal. Overall, compromising has to take place on both sides. While compromises may not be equal, nobody should totally give up his own reality to live entirely in someone else's.

Dreams into Goals

Everything starts out as a dream. Goals and dreams differ in that people often don't act on their dreams, usually because the dreams seem too impractical and ambitious to be realized. Goals require action on your part to make them happen. Your goals might initially start out very broad, based on your needs and wishes; they basically represent your ideals or dreams. They can then be broken down into smaller, attainable goals so that you can take action to make them come true. Your relationship progresses as long as you move in the direction of your goals, however slowly.

START WITH YOUR DREAMS

Many people have difficulty imagining that their dreams can come true. They often say, "Our relationship can change only if my partner becomes a different person. So what's the point of dreaming?" In fact, your problems do not stem from only one partner; they are a product of both of you. You would both have to be different people in order to have a different relationship.

Remember that since you live in a relationship system, any change in you will affect your partner. You need patience and perseverance to continue pushing ahead while your partner does not seem to change. Eventually, the changes in you can create positive, desired changes in your partner.

You and your partner may have been unable to meet each other's needs in some very fundamental ways. You can change, and so can your relationship. Be realistic, though. Start slowly, and you can eventually turn your dreams into big goals with small, doable steps; even small changes make a difference over time. You can find ways to feel more satisfied in your relationship and to go happily into the future. Use your dreams to formulate your goals for continued progress.

PERSONAL GOALS VS. PARTNERSHIP GOALS

Relationship goals include personal goals about your own behavior in your relationship, your partner's personal goals for her own behavior, and shared goals that you and your partner work on together. You cannot make goals for your partner to work on without her full participation and agreement.

Two general types of goals help you to meet relationship needs: your own personal goals and your partnership goals. "I will yell less at my partner" is a personal, individual goal. You alone work on your personal goals and maintain responsibility for reaching them. Personal goals often include checking your own attitudes, values, and behaviors. With your partner's consent and participation, you can also work on partnership goals. "We will develop an anger contract to make our heated discussions more productive" demonstrates a partnership goal. Both of you must work together to reach partnership goals.

If your partner cannot see the logic in working together on relationship goals, stick to developing and working on your personal goals for now. Maybe you can make logical arguments to get some of your needs met. When your logic does not help, you can pick your battles more carefully. For example, weigh the importance of such things as whether or not your partner combs his hair before going out against whether he is loyal and dependable. Does looking disheveled in front of neighbors on a walk around the block feel the same as his arriving looking unkempt at your workplace? Compromise can help your relationship move beyond such issues and focus on the ones of most importance to you. If lack of interest on your partner's part or unwillingness to set goals and work toward a more fulfilling union continues, you may want to reconsider the relationship, a possibility we discuss in chapter 12. For now, you can still make progress by working on your own personal goals in order to get your needs met.

At this point, focus on needs that remain unmet after you have clearly and specifically stated them to your partner. To move away from being stuck in these areas, think creatively about your relationship and what you could do to get what you need. Your partner may have any combination of AS characteristics, but regardless of her unique traits, you can work to develop deeper intimacy. Go slowly and considerately to avoid undue stress for your partner, but be persistent. This book presents opportunities to develop and revise your goals, to work on problem areas in your relationship, and to get more of your relationship needs met. Let's take a closer look at how to break your needs down into specific, doable goals that you can achieve in the short run.

Personal Goals. When focusing on personal goals, consider your needs and look for ways to change your own thoughts or actions to get them met. Think about actions you can take right now to get closer to meeting a particular need. It also helps to consider feedback you've received from your partner about relationship issues that he believes you contribute to. This may increase your chances of getting your own needs met by helping him see that it's not only about you and your needs.

Perhaps you could make it your goal to involve your partner more or to present your ideas in more supportive ways that might be easier for her to accept. Your partner may have difficulties with communication, as we have seen over and over with Asperger's syndrome. Can your own communication within your relationship improve? Can your personal goal involve helping your partner with communication difficulties or being more patient about them? (Chapter 7, which is dedicated to effective relationship communication, may also help you discover helpful areas to work on and what types of goals may be realistic.)

EXERCISE 5.2   Developing Personal Goals

Consider your dreams as goals you can work on, rather than fantasies that will never come true. You will develop short-term goals for yourself in your relationship that you can begin to work on immediately to get your needs met. Table 5.3, "Your Dreams into Goals," offers examples of translating your dreams for your relationship into specific, action-oriented goals for yourself. (You can do this exercise again to create goals for your partnership; just have the third column be "Partnership Goals" instead of "Personal Goals.")

1. Use your list of prioritized needs from exercise 5.1 to make a list of dreams that represent how you would like your relationship to be. You can also use specific relationship situations that you need changed. State these dreams in broad terms. "I want more fun and spontaneity in my relationship" is an example of a very general, broad dream. Try to avoid dreams that require you or your partner to change who you are, fundamentally: "I want to feel more connected" versus "I want my partner to be the life of the party."

2. On a page that is separated into three columns, put your dreams in the first column. Label the columns "Dreams," "Wish List," and "Personal Goals." In the "Wish List" column, break each dream down into two or three small changes that might begin to move you toward your dream. What would be a fun or spontaneous act that would help you feel a little happier? Does your wish list include going places with your partner, or adding new and different foods to your weekly menu? List these in column 2.

3. Break each wish down into more specific goals that you can begin to work on today. If your dream is to have more fun and spontaneity in your relationship and your partner shows little interest in going out, it will be necessary to go at a very slow pace as you advance toward a larger social goal. Perhaps your personal goal begins with your going out to have fun with friends occasionally without your partner. Write at least one way that you can change your own thoughts or behaviors to step closer to the change you wish for.

4. State your goal positively and clearly, and make it measureable. "My goal is to go out and do more things" does not specify how to make this happen. Who will take action? How often or when? What will you do? "I will go out with friends once per month" shows a clear action for you to take to reach this goal. It also states the goal more positively than "I can't stand never going out with our friends." Start with once per month and add on gradually to get as close to your ideal goal for going out as your partnership can handle.

5. Review your goals periodically. Develop new goals each time the current ones become a new way of being in your relationship.

TABLE 5.3   Your Dreams into Goals

Dream	Wish List	Personal Goals
I want more physical affection in our relationship.	Hugs Holding hands Cuddling	I won't force my partner to hug or hold my hand; I'll ask for a hug once a day.
I want to go out and socialize together more often.	Go out with friends. Have friends over to our place. Go to parties when we're invited.	I'll invite her once a week to a place she enjoys. I'll go out with a friend at least once a month.

I want help around the house and more equal distribution of housework.	Help with: Cleaning the kitchen Vacuuming Laundry	I will not criticize the way she folds laundry or the way she fills the dishwasher.

Base your goals on the change you want to see in your relationship. Consider ideas for personal actions to make the change happen and how you will know it when you see it.

You need to break goals down into smaller steps for your partnership too. They should be specific, measureable, realistic (achievable), and time sensitive. You and your partner may share a similar vision, but without a plan for realizing your relationship dreams, you may both wait for them to come true...and wait...and wait.

Partnership Goals. Start at a pace that you and your partner can actually keep. Now that you know more about Asperger's syndrome and your partner, take his difficulty with change and need for predictability into account. For example, small, specific goals to include planned spontaneity may help get things started and create changes in this area of your relationship. Then, the more your partner spends time with certain friends, the more comfortable he may feel around them; you may even be able to invite them over spontaneously for some future night of socializing. In the meantime, start with very small steps, such as those in table 5.3. For now, compromising on spontaneity in order to have some fun pulls your relationship in a positive direction.

EXERCISE 5.3   Developing Partnership Goals

As you brainstorm ideas with your partner, listen and respond to her point of view. Some agreement is better than none. If the trend heads in a positive direction, it is positive.

1.   Working separately, write down five unmet needs (use table 5.1 for ideas). You will each come up with your own, possibly resulting in up to ten areas of concern between you.

2. For each need, name at least two specific changes you want to see. For example, if you list communication as a need, you may have specific issues in mind. Maybe you want to focus on how little your partner shares with you about his day or that his only dinner conversation revolves around his special interest. Name the change you want to see in your relationship.

3. Share your relationship needs with each other and brainstorm to find mutually agreeable goals. Remember to include your partner's needs and ways to meet them. If you cannot agree on certain goals, keep trying to find common goals that you can agree on. Focus on where you can compromise, even a little bit. Other needs and goals can be revisited another time.

4. Write down the goals that you both agree on. Make your goals small, specific, clear, and understandable. For example, under the point stating that your partner does not share enough with you about his day, perhaps you can both agree on five minutes of daily conversation where you each get a turn to share facts about your day.

You can make a chart for you and your partner similar to table 5.3 if you both want one. The visual aid often works to keep the partner with AS involved and to clarify the process for him. Try to keep your goals balanced and realistic. Going out once a month or spending five minutes of forced conversation is probably not ideal for either one of you. Every step counts when you are changing unhealthy patterns and working toward a more satisfying relationship. Your relationship will change in a positive direction over time, and you will have the opportunity to change and add more goals.

Compromise for Change

Your AS partner may want your relationship to continue on as it is now, while you, like many non-AS partners, value continued change. A compromise position for change in a relationship between someone with Asperger's and a neurotypical partner involves change that continues very gradually, not enough for you to feel completely stagnant but not so much that it feels overwhelming to your partner. Make sure to clue your partner in to the whole process. Otherwise, she may feel that you constantly keep moving the target every time she reaches it, rather than understand your expectations for your relationship to continuously change and grow.

Unless your partner agrees on goals and steps to achieve them with you, the goals you work on right now can include only your own personal goals to get what you need. Hopefully, even a reluctant partner will gain interest and step up to work with you toward relationship goals. Continue to invite your partner to join you in working on your needs and goals, but too much pressure may cause withdrawal rather than cooperation. For the time being, a basic outline of what you want to achieve in your relationship and some short-term goals will help you begin working toward change right away.

Can Your Relationship Really Change?

Realistically, some things can change and some cannot. Change rarely comes easily, and rigidity in the face of change can represent a characteristic of Asperger's syndrome. In reality, there may be some needs that you or your partner cannot meet for each other. Perhaps you can consider what you truly need, and compromise so that your needs can be met either with or without relying specifically on your partner. For example, you may have to rely more on family and friends for spontaneity and variety. If too many needs remain unmet, you may need a counselor to help you sort them out and work with you and your partner to make necessary changes.

Change takes patience and perseverance. Understanding the nature of AS and knowing more about your partner can help in finding ways to compensate, learn, and grow together. The point to remember is that people can change. In my profession, I help people change ineffective thoughts and behavior, or unsatisfying issues in their lives. I could not continue to do this if I didn't believe with certainty that it's possible.

You do not have to change yourself or your needs. What must change is the balance in your relationship so that it becomes more satisfying and offers more and more of what you hope for. To achieve this, you may have to change some of your behavior or expectations, and some of the ways you think about your partner and your relationship.

Points to Keep in Mind

Getting your needs met remains one of the biggest and most important changes to come about from working on your partnership. But if you keep doing the same things to get your needs met, you will keep getting the same results. That's why you're reading this book and why it was written. Perhaps you feel ready to make a deeper change.

You have developed initial goals for making needed changes between you and your partner. These goals stem from your needs and desires, and represent a blueprint for enriching your relationship. Turning your dreams into action-oriented goals can help bridge a gap in understanding between you and your partner with AS.

Your partner may need only short-term, doable goals; dream goals may not make sense to your practical-minded partner. It's important to accept his point of view. Your goals can still be attainable and should focus on what you can do to get your needs met. Think about at least one thing you can do right now, today, to move closer to a goal. When your relationship moves toward your short- or long-term dreams and goals, both you and your partner move together toward a common vision.

CHAPTER 6

Dealing with Anger

Anger is a signal, and one worth listening to.

—Harriet Lerner

Anger is a major obstacle for people with Asperger's syndrome and their partners. When couples come to me for help, they often come loaded with built-up disappointment and frustration. This much negativity blocks understanding and progress in therapy.

For non-AS partners, anger often results from unmet expectations or misunderstandings in relation to a partner with AS. When you don't realize you're dealing with Asperger's or don't understand the condition, resentment and misunderstandings may be more pronounced. The personality traits in Asperger's syndrome can be upsetting, especially when you believe your partner purposely antagonizes and upsets you.

From the other side, some people with AS remain rational through it all, but many become easily agitated and blow up, even as adults. Anger is not one of the symptoms of Asperger's syndrome per se. Many conditions overlap with AS, such as anxiety or heightened sensitivity (see chapter 11), and they can increase agitation. As a result, people with Asperger's often struggle with managing emotions that agitate and frustrate them, so these emotions come out as anger. Emotions in AS often work like an on-or-off switch, as opposed to a dimmer. Someone with AS may also react with intense anxiety or anger to a social situation or to a painful sensory experience, such as loud noises or bright lights.

Anger as a Relationship Signal

Anger signals upset and displeasure; it signals that needs or desires are not being met in some way. Working together in a healthy relationship takes patience and a kind of tolerance that may be hard to find when love and positive feelings get buried under negativity or anger. Anger can be one of the most destructive emotions for a relationship, if left unchecked. Both you and your partner with AS may feel let down, disillusioned, and angry, but for very different reasons. Hopefully you picked up this book because you want to move beyond anger and connect lovingly with your partner.

According to Aaron Beck (1988), founder of cognitive therapy, in *Love Is Never Enough: How Couples Can Overcome Misunderstandings, Resolve Conflicts, and Solve Relationship Problems through Cognitive Therapy*, anger causes a sense of pressure to do something. What you do when you feel angry at your partner or when your partner with AS expresses anger at you affects your relationship in many ways. Your anger can make change happen, but too much anger for too long can be destructive to you and your relationship.

Growing Resentment

Many ex-partners mention that if they had known they were dealing with Asperger's syndrome before the breakup, the relationship might have survived; they would have understood and worked differently with their partners. These partners were unable to get past the resentment and anger that grew between them and their AS partners. Both your anger and that of your partner must be validated and taken seriously.

Roots of Your Anger

Certain AS behaviors seem to prompt anger in a neurotypical partner. A partner with Asperger's syndrome can appear cool and calm in the face of your upset feelings, and can seemingly ignore verbal and nonverbal cues about your need for comfort. Your partner may seem rigid and uncaring. You may find her comments inappropriate, embarrassing, or infuriating. Some non-AS partners compensate for their AS partners' relative weaknesses by handling everything themselves, from finances to household chores to caring for the children. You may not feel that you can trust your partner with these responsibilities. This can lead to resentment when it seems as if you cannot depend on your partner to share fully in your relationship.

Roots of Your Partner's Anger

Partners with Asperger's syndrome who are struggling in a relationship often complain about the neurotypical partner's nearly constant anger. Over time, your anger makes your partner angry too. He believed in your unconditional love and may feel confused at your anger and disappointment. To someone with AS, your anger can seem unpredictable and may end up feeling like a lack of love. One client, Talia, became very angry at her partner and yelled, "I can't stand you right now." "Now the truth comes out," he responded, "You can't stand me."

Sometimes the angrier you get, the more your partner withdraws or gets angry as well, because life feels so uncomfortable with you. After all, he's the same guy you said you loved; he may not understand how you can love him and be angry with him at the same time. Being literal minded, even in his emotional life, your partner may stop making an effort in the relationship when faced with too much anger, feeling that to continue trying is useless. Love, like life, can be black and white to a person with AS. You either love him or not. And if you do, why are you so angry so much of the time?

Emotional Outbursts and Meltdowns

Meltdowns occur when someone feels overwhelmed and has difficulty managing or dealing with the emotions. For a person with Asperger's syndrome, a meltdown can include increases in AS behaviors, such as rigidity, difficulty calming down, and physical agitation.

Keeping anger inside until it cannot be suppressed any longer can result in an emotional outburst. Trying to get your point across and feeling that your partner is inattentive because she just did that same annoying thing again can also lead to emotional outbursts of anger.

Meltdowns and outbursts serve to alert partners to serious feelings, but usually end up being hurtful and distressing. Your partner with AS may feel as if he walks a tightrope to keep your "irrational demands" from flaring up, and you may work just as hard at avoiding situations that may lead to his meltdowns. Angry outbursts often end up with both partners feeling hurt and vulnerable. Such displays may lead to a beneficial discussion later, but you can get to a valuable discussion without a blowup or a meltdown.

What upsets your partner may not always make sense to you, just as things that make you upset may seem irrational from her viewpoint. It is untrue that people with AS do not feel. Often, their sensitivity and desire to do the right thing touches them so deeply that they either get very upset or totally withdraw. While your partner may be calm, cool, and collected when you believe that being emotional is appropriate, she may have strong emotional reactions at other times in your relationship.

Emotional outbursts and meltdowns signal the breakdown of important communication; someone feels misunderstood or not taken care of in some way. When either of you reacts with anger, it can be difficult for the other not to retaliate. If your relationship dynamic contains frequent emotional outbursts or meltdowns that seem out of control, one or both of you may benefit from working with a mental health professional.

Ways to Deal with Anger

Holding in what makes you feel angry remains counterproductive, whether you do it because you dislike confrontation, you don't want to hurt your partner's feelings, you fear your partner's reaction, or you're just plain tired of fighting. Anger does not go away by avoiding its expression, and doing so may lead to long-term resentment toward your partner and depression in you.

People with AS don't necessarily have the same need to express emotions as many non-AS people do. They often prefer to discuss the issue or cause of the emotion, such as anger, in order to resolve it, but do not necessarily need to put a label on it or talk about anger specifically. A male with AS told me recently that he doesn't need to express anger; he needs to address the issue that makes him angry, and once addressed, the anger is irrelevant. Logically, if we deal with the issue at the heart of the anger, do we need to express the anger itself?

The way you express your anger makes it useful or harmful in your relationship. Venting anger to blow off steam and make your partner feel bad usually ends up hurting both of you. Anger can be useful if you pay attention to the feeling in order to understand your needs and let your partner know them. The goal in any long-term relationship is not to hurt your partner, but to work toward deeper understanding between the two of you.

You might think that your anger is obvious from your mood, tone, or facial expressions. But people with AS can have difficulty interpreting nonverbal language and the emotions of others. The more extreme reactions, such as yelling and crying, may be obvious to all concerned but can also seem irrational or hysterical to your partner. Yet she may not even pick up on your more subtle expressions of anger. Facial cues such as frowning, furrowing your brow, or staring may not be read accurately or even at all. Plus, it may not mean much for your partner to know that you are angry if she has no idea what caused your anger, or how to prevent or change it.

Before you're tempted to minimize your feelings of anger, realize that the needs your anger signals require expression. Expressing your needs gives your partner the opportunity to either change his behavior or attitude to better meet them, or to help you to understand his side of the issue. Either one of these reactions can help you to better understand yourself and your partner. Repressing anger and not expressing your needs offers no opportunity for resolution.

Indirect Expressions of Anger

Shari came to her appointment upset because her boyfriend with AS, Curtis, had stayed home the evening before, when she went to the hospital to visit her mom. She painfully recalled patiently having sat all day, on her day off, in the hospital with his grandmother before they even lived together. She felt that if he loved her, he would have come with her to see her mom. The first time she asked him, she said, "I'm visiting my mom after work tonight. Should I wait for you, so you can come too?" When he replied that it was fine not to wait, she tried again: "It's really no problem; I can wait if you want me to," to which he replied again that it was fine for her to go ahead on her own. She was furious that he didn't volunteer to go; it was the "right" thing to do, and she "obviously" wanted him to go with her. "I asked him twice. That should tell him it's important," she exclaimed.

Until we talked about this in more depth, Shari did not consider her partner's logical perspective. Asking a question twice, if interpreted logically, can mean that you didn't hear or understand the answer the first time. It helps to make a specific request of your partner; inference fails to work nearly as well. This holds true in most relationships, but even more so if your partner has Asperger's. As this example illustrates, asking directly for what you want can help you to avoid feeling disappointed. If you ask directly and your partner disappoints you, it presents an opportunity to discuss the issue and come to a compromise or resolution.

Shari's anger built to a fever pitch, and she continued yelling about it the next day, but Curtis couldn't understand the problem. When he offered no response because he couldn't think of a rational response to her seemingly irrational behavior, she became even angrier and accused him of emotional abuse. These misunderstandings happen often in partnerships where one person has AS. Since the behavior makes little sense to the AS partner in the first place, he may experience it as unpredictable and therefore avoid responding.

Your expectation in this moment may be exactly the opposite of what comes naturally for your partner. After being upset, your AS partner may need time alone to recharge, while you may want reassurance, a hug, something that helps you to feel connected. In this case, Shari wanted an apology, which came in the form of flowers at work; through past experience with her, Curtis knew that when he sends flowers after a fight, she feels better. It did make Shari feel better, but this sequence failed to help him to understand what went wrong or how to fix it in the future.

When expressed constructively, your anger can help your partner to understand your expectations as well as help her to be more accommodating. Some partners express concern about showing anger toward their AS partners, because they feel that their partners "can't help" their behavior. Understanding your partner and her Asperger's syndrome doesn't make all behavior acceptable. People with AS do have a difficult time in relationships, but you need to give them some credit for being capable of working toward change too.

Many people, especially women, tend to feel guilty about expressing anger. We are sometimes taught from an early age that expressing personal needs is selfish or that doing so hurts the other person. Unnecessary or excessive guilt can cause some people to hold back expressions of anger or requests for what they need. You don't want to hurt your partner, but not letting him know what you need offers no opportunity for him to provide it for you.

Your Personal Coping Strategies

How do you cope with anger? Do you try not to show it? Do you explode at your partner? Do you take a walk and think it through before bringing it up for discussion? Does guilt block you from bringing it up?

You may find that some of your current coping strategies work well. If so, you can highlight and work on them so that they become stronger and even more useful. If you find that your coping strategies don't really help you to get what you're looking for, you can work on adopting new, healthier ways of expressing anger.

EXERCISE 6.1   Anger Coping Skills

This exercise explores anger triggers and personal coping strategies. You will strengthen strategies that work well and change strategies that don't. Table 6.1, "Coping with Anger," offers an example of how your completed exercise might look.

1. Label your page with four columns: "Anger Triggers," "How I Cope," "Consequences," and "New Strategy."

2. In the first column, make a list of situations in your relationship that make you angry. There may be many; for now, list no more than five.

3. Think about how you tend to react to the behavior or situation, the way you cope currently. Write this down in the second column.

4. In the third column, write about what typically happens in this situation, the consequence of your coping strategy. Does it work? If so, keep it as a strategy. If not, think about how to change your coping strategy so that it works better in your relationship.

5. Can you think of at least one different way to cope with your anger? Write it in the "New Strategy" column.

6. Next time the situation happens, try your new response. If your new way of coping helps, continue to refine and use it. If it does not appear to matter after you've tried a few times, brainstorm and try another new response.

7. Have your partner do her own anger coping chart, and discuss your charts with each other. She may not know how she feels or how her emotions come across. You can help her to become aware of her anger and how she copes. You can both help each other come up with more helpful responses.

TABLE 6.1   Coping with Anger

Anger Triggers	How I Cope	Consequences	New Strategy
He eats his macaroni and cheese alone before dinner and then isn't hungry.	I stopped yelling like I used to. Now I just sit alone and have my dinner.	We almost never eat together, and I feel angry and lonely.	I'll offer a small appetizer to hold him over and discuss sharing meals.

He spends evenings on the computer after dinner.	I spend the evening on my computer, but I'm fuming inside.	There's more and more distance between us.	I can invite him to do something else we both enjoy.
He goes on and on about his opinions.	I get very tense. I try to change the subject and sometimes just walk away.	He doesn't pay attention to me and seems to withdraw more and more.	I'll put my hand on his shoulder when I need him to get to the point more quickly.
He yells because the dishwasher isn't loaded a certain way.	We end up screaming at each other and can never agree.	One of us usually ends up storming off, and we stay mad for a while.	I'll have him load the dishwasher his way, or do it myself when he's busy.

If your partner doesn't complete this exercise, you can still benefit from learning about what triggers your own anger and why. It may also be helpful for you to complete the exercise once more, writing down your partner's anger triggers and coping strategies as you perceive them. Here's a note of caution: when you fill out any exercise as you think someone else would, it's not the same as their doing it on their own. You cannot know for certain what your partner would say, so you have to leave room for error and not take your perspective as fact. Still, completing this exercise according to your perceptions may help you to focus on your partner and be better able to recognize her anger triggers in order to avoid them, de-escalate potentially destructive interactions, or both.

Try to think of new strategies that don't rely on your partner's involvement, such as the example in the previous chart of preparing an appetizer or changing the way you load the dishwasher. If your strategies involve something your partner needs to do, such as understand a new nonverbal signal for when to stop talking, you have to clue him in and get him on board with the plan. Suggest possible new responses at a time when he feels relaxed and can be receptive to constructive feedback. Discover what works for the two of you in your particular relationship.

You can learn to handle your own anger responses and have a positive effect on your relationship, whether or not your partner chooses to participate. As long as productive work remains, you can keep working, with or without your partner.

KNOW THE TRIGGERS

Knowing what triggers anger in you or your partner can allow you both to be proactive about preventing potential outbursts and destructive fights, by making necessary changes or adjustments. Coping better with distressing emotions begins with understanding your triggers and reactions, and the strengths or weaknesses you possess to deal with them. Once anger gets triggered, taking action to address it helps avoid its escalating to the point of an outburst or meltdown. Developing new, more positive, responses to situations that upset you will go a long way toward making your relationship feel good to be part of.

Healthy Ways to Express Anger

The healthiest way for you to deal with anger in your relationship involves discussing causes and solutions with your partner, and resolving issues that trigger your anger. This is difficult in any relationship and, as we now know, may be even more difficult in yours. The chapter on communication (chapter 7) includes tips and exercises for discussing issues that make you angry and for expressing your needs to your partner.

RESOLVING DISAGREEMENTS

Resolving conflict requires compromise. Look for compromise positions where you can both "win," and remember to use the 1-to-10 scale from chapter 5. You can use an emotional thermometer in the same way. Some people use a large picture of a thermometer and draw anger as it moves up the scale toward a fever. In situations with no potential for compromise, take turns "winning." Meet your partner in the middle whenever possible, but of course don't compromise your values, your safety, or your well being.

One couple was in a quandary about an upcoming party in Vermont. The party was for a mutual friend whom neither partner wanted to disappoint. The partner with Asperger's syndrome was looking forward to the weekend in the mountains and seeing a few friends that the couple seldom got to see. At the same time, she dreaded the large party in a noisy restaurant with other people she didn't know well. After a lengthy discussion, the couple agreed that they would schedule a weekend away for just the two of them and offer to take their mutual friend out to dinner another time, when there would be fewer people and they could choose the restaurant.

A MODEL FOR RESOLVING CONFLICTS

The following model may help in resolving disagreements between you and your partner with AS.

1. *Identify the problem.* Offer logical reasons why compromise is necessary, so that your AS partner may be more willing to help find an agreeable solution.

2. *Listen to your partner's point of view.* Take both of your perspectives into account. Write down points of agreement and disagreement, and address them one by one.

3. *Brainstorm with your partner.* Write all possible solutions, regardless of their feasibility. Start with points of agreement so that you both feel progress. Find mutually agreeable ideas and continue until you reach a reasonable compromise.

4. *Review your possible solutions.* Write the pros and cons of each one.

5. *Choose a mutually acceptable solution.* Make it one with the highest probability of success. You probably both have to give up something to arrive at a good compromise.

6. *Try your new solution.* Make specific goals to cover who will do what and when, as well as what happens if the solution breaks down.

7. *Evaluate.* If you find that your solution isn't working, initiate a new discussion to make mutually agreeable revisions.

MORE WAYS TO DEAL WITH ANGER

The strong emotional reactions that anger triggers can make it difficult to think calmly and rationally and to fight fairly. Before expressing anger constructively, we often need to calm the initial emotional response. Sometimes the energy of anger builds up and needs a physical release. You can release negative energy in a positive way through relaxation or by participating in a distracting activity. Physical activity often helps us to let go of negative feelings and develop more positive energy. Choices for releasing negativity can vary greatly and include activities as diverse as these:

* Listening to music

* Spending time alone

* Practicing deep breathing

* Working out

* Gardening

* Playing a musical instrument or singing

* Riding your bike

* Walking or running

* Doing yoga

* Engaging in any other enjoyable physical activity

Most of us cannot engage in a worthwhile discussion about our anger until we get the raw emotion somewhat under control. You can also help your partner by being on the lookout for his increasing symptoms of anger, such as turning red, rocking, pacing, or repetitively expressing upset thoughts. When you recognize certain triggers and cues as a sign of increasing anger, you can help your partner by encouraging him to use his particular relaxation techniques, calming distractions, or physical activity. You can also do this for yourself, and perhaps your partner can be enlisted to help you as well.

Once you feel somewhat calmer, you can have a more rewarding conversation that might actually change the destructive dance in your relationship. Deal with anger as close to when you experience it as possible, rather than letting resentment build up. Over time, you can learn to react differently to your partner's behaviors and to recognize anger cues sooner so that you can prevent a blowup.

Establishing clear rules can help manage anger in your relationship. When the anger lessens enough to be discussed, having firm and clear rules for arguing helps couples keep their emotions under better control. Helpful rules might include:

* Keeping voices at a usual level

* Maintaining respect for each other at all times

* Avoiding name-calling

These are just a few basic guidelines to avoid allowing arguments to escalate. The chapter on communication (chapter 7) presents additional suggestions for making your rules explicit and your discussions more productive. Until you can both follow these basic guidelines, time-outs may be needed to lower the tension, and you can try again at a specified interval after the time-outs.

It may take time for you and your partner to get to a place where you can tolerate difficult discussions, and some issues may continue to present problems. When you can't resolve an issue, don't "agree to disagree" yet continue to hold on to resentment. There may be disagreement between the two of you that you agree to live with, but you can still respect each other's differences and points of view. When you can't resolve a disagreement with your partner or move beyond it, you might find it helpful to work through it in your journal or to find outside support. If you need more support than friends or family members can give you, counseling may be needed.

Points to Keep in Mind

Understanding Asperger's syndrome may help lower the intensity of your anger toward your partner and refocus your energy into loving and understanding her. This doesn't mean that you should never be angry. Be aware of what makes you angry and what you do when you feel angry. Be mindful of the way you communicate anger and the way you accept your partner's anger. Angry feelings should be heeded and responded to as important communication signals. Express anger considerately and directly; ask for what you want and need.

Dealing with anger constructively helps you and your partner move past negative feelings into a deeper connection. Over time, your past hurt and resentment will arrive at a more positive place, where you can continue working productively on your relationship. Listening to your partner's concerns and communicating effectively will help you and your partner as you move forward in your life together. The next chapter explores these topics further.

CHAPTER 7

Communication That Works

The single biggest problem in communication is the illusion that it has taken place.

—George Bernard Shaw

Good communication is an essential building block toward a fulfilling relationship. Communication is often one of the primary areas affecting relationships that include a partner with Asperger's syndrome. The way you and your partner communicate feelings, needs, and expectations affects your relationship in many ways. Uncertainty between you and your partner can contribute to misunderstandings and negative effects on both of you and on your relationship. This makes it important for you two to understand each others' communication and interaction styles.

The Way You Communicate

Patterns of communication and interaction within a relationship begin to develop from the start. The best time to set up your ideal relationship communication is at the outset, before patterns develop. People with AS often demonstrate a great deal of difficulty in making changes once things become part of a usual and expected routine. Patterns of communication can change, but, once developed, change may occur gradually and sometimes painstakingly.

Relating in the Long Term

Many people with Asperger's syndrome learn relationship communication by observing others who appear to be socially skilled. Learning scripts from TV shows and movies can help at first, by supplying good one-liners and questions to get things started. Ryan uses lines and situations from the TV show *Seinfeld* when he's uncertain of what to say or do in his relationship. He often finds parallel situations that help him figure out what to do or say in particular relationship moments. But someone like Ryan, who takes cues from imitation, may be stumped by unique questions or responses; he might not have a comeback or be able to think of one spontaneously. Your partner may not have a way to relate to you romantically in a long-term way. It can be very upsetting for both of you when communication and interaction start to break down and you wonder why.

An AS partner may experience a meltdown in the face of an unexpected situation. For example, if you arrange dinner for six o'clock, your partner expects dinner at six. Having dinner an hour later than expected can turn the anxiety switch on and result in a meltdown. It helps for your partner to learn that an appropriate script in such a situation might be to say, "I have trouble when you change the dinner plans," or "Please try to give me more time when you make changes." Having a script like this one may help the next time you have dinner ready an hour late.

When your partner's anxiety shoots up over a quick change, she may not remember her script the first few times, though she can gradually learn to manage this. But she may not necessarily realize automatically that the same script should be used if you invite someone else to dinner, if the location of dinner changes, or if you change the expected menu. The similarity in circumstances may seem obvious to you, but your AS partner may have trouble generalizing. For some people with AS, each variation in your plan may need a specific script, and each script will take time to learn and use in the right critical moment.

Using scripts may seem mechanical, but you can view them more favorably when you remember that we all learn many social skills through scripts. Children don't naturally say "please" and "thank you" unless encouraged to do so over and over again. Your AS partner is not a child, but may need time to develop certain skills that you take for granted.

While we're on the subject, power cards may also be a helpful strategy for your partner to deal with unexpected changes. The size of a business card, a "power card" has a set of steps for dealing with a situation on one side. The other side usually displays a picture that is closely associated with the situation to be handled. For example, one side could have a picture of a gymnast, and the other side could list three possible scripts for flexible thinking. New applications to help people with scheduling, organizing, and even dealing with change are coming out rapidly for smartphones and tablet computers—not a cure but helpful for people who learn best this way.

Many partners who come for help later in their relationships wish they had realized much earlier the need to spell out their expectations and to develop scripts and rules, instead of quietly fuming over the years whenever expectations had gone unmet. It may seem obvious to you that when you bring in seven heavy packages of groceries, your partner should offer to help, but without direct communication, this may not be obvious to your partner. Indirect communication also makes it difficult for either of you to realize the support the two of you might need with relating in order to bring both of you more satisfaction.

Types of Communication

No matter what you do, you communicate. Even by saying nothing, you say something. We communicate through spoken or written words, actions, gestures, or other body language. Verbal language includes typical speech as well as humor, sarcasm, and double meanings. People with AS often have difficulty with nonliteral speech; they expect words to mean what they say. Letting your partner know that talking to him is like "banging my head against a wall" might seem insane to him. He may wonder, "Why would you bang your head against a wall?"

Nonverbal language makes up a significant portion of communication. It includes eye contact, face and hand gestures, and other body language, such as how close or far you stand to people when you speak with them. As with words that are not literal, someone with AS can have a great deal of difficulty understanding communication that uses no words at all. People with Asperger's can best understand clear and direct spoken or written language.

Verbal Communication

People with Asperger's syndrome may have a hard time making small talk or smoothly exchanging dialog in a conversation. Your partner may need help with understanding the logic of social chitchat and may need to get some coaching on when, why, and how to make polite conversation. Problems may especially arise in unstructured situations that hold no predictable question-and-answer sequence, such as, "How was your day?" "Not bad. How was yours?" It can get much more complicated when someone casually asks your partner, "What kind of work do you do?" For example, she may take such a question as an invitation to discuss her biochemical research variables in great detail.

The highly focused interests of some people with Asperger's may lead to highly focused, limited conversations. Offering briefer explanations to specific questions, such as queries about work, may seem obvious to you, but your partner may need support to learn this. Communication must be open and direct, or your partner may have no idea what you want or need. Be as specific and clear as possible so that your communication makes sense to your partner. He may experience you as unrealistically wanting him to read your mind.

Sometimes I make mistakes in this regard too. Recently, a woman with AS came in for a first therapy appointment. I introduced myself and asked her to take a seat in the waiting room for a few minutes. When I passed the waiting room a couple of minutes later, she was still standing;

she said she wasn't sure where I meant for her to sit. Most people come in and take any one of the seven or eight seats in the waiting area, but this woman needed more specific instructions to understand my expectation.

Nonverbal Communication

Nonverbal language proves difficult for many people with Asperger's syndrome. Your partner may lack understanding of personal space or other nonverbal body language and gestures. Your partner may not interpret your cold, hard stare; your pout; or even your teeth gritting as anything to pay attention to.

Recently I phoned someone with AS and reached him on his cell phone while he was eating breakfast in a restaurant with his partner. In spite of the fact that they were out dining together, he insisted that this was a good time to talk. As we were talking, I heard a great deal of coughing in the background. I asked if that was his partner coughing, and he replied, "Yes, it is. She's choking, which happens a lot when she drinks too quickly, but she chooses to gulp her orange juice anyway."

His willingness to resume the conversation concerned me, and I kept asking if his partner was okay (which he did not ask her) and whether he needed to do anything to help her out. Fortunately his partner stopped choking so that we could resume the conversation. I was stuck on the choking situation, whereas he had experienced this before and believed that everything would work itself out without there being a need to focus on it. I have no idea whether his partner wants him to do anything differently during future choking episodes, but if so, she will have to spell it out clearly for him.

EXERCISE 7.1 Translating Nonverbal Communication

In this exercise, you translate your nonverbal communication so that your partner can understand you. Your nonverbal communication chart should look something like table 7.1, "Nonverbal Communication Translation."

1. Observe yourself and your partner. Write down the different things you try to say nonverbally and how you try to say them.

2. Translate your nonverbal language into words to tell your partner.

3. Make a list or chart for your partner of your nonverbal expressions and what they mean. It can help even more if you add a picture column that shows what you look like when you engage in these various nonverbal behaviors.

TABLE 7.1   Nonverbal Communication Translation

When I...	It means I am...
Roll my eyes or look away	Annoyed or bored
Bang on the table or say mean things	Frustrated or angry
Sit close to you on the sofa	Hoping you will stay next to me

Do not expect to offer your partner a translation chart and proceed smoothly through your time together. This is only the beginning, a small offering. Ideally, you will need to verbalize as much as possible, rather than require your partner to read your subtle body language or secret gestural codes.

Your partner communicates nonverbally too, but she may not be aware that she does so or what her nonverbal language communicates to you. Doing the previous exercise might also help your partner to become more aware of her own nonverbal communication and what it means in interactions with you.

Effective Communication

As we've discussed, healthy communication involves asking for and getting what you need, and taking steps to find solutions to relationship problems that benefit both of you. Further skills for communicating effectively with your AS partner involve active listening and learning to offer constructive feedback.

Active Listening

How you listen to your partner will be a major factor in whether or not he feels understood and taken seriously. Active listening involves paying close attention and letting your partner know that you truly hear him. You can do this by:

* Asking questions in order to understand his perspective, rather than listening for where you can find flaws in his argument. Say, "Tell me more about that," or ask, "What was that like for you?" instead of asking, "How did that make you feel?"

* Listening without interrupting or becoming defensive. Try to do this even if you do not want to hear it, have heard it twenty times before, or disagree.

* Reflecting back what you hear. Paraphrase your partner so that he knows you're listening and really trying to understand his point of view. He'll be more likely to follow your logic if you start from his perspective and lead him to understand yours.

Relationship Rules and Expectations

One of the biggest difficulties in relationships where one partner has Asperger's syndrome is when the relationship rules and expectations don't get explicitly communicated. As mentioned in chapter 2, the hidden curriculum in relationships eludes many people with AS. The lack of explicit rules and predictability can lead to frustration in intimate partnerships. While you may see your partner as insensitive, she may, in fact, be oversensitive to the unpredictability of being your partner. This can be highly stressful for someone who may already be struggling with the unpredictability of your complicated emotional world.

EXERCISE 7.2 Make Your Rules Explicit

You may not even realize that you have rules until your partner breaks one and upsets you. Relationship rules that you may find intuitive can be problematic for your partner. Be explicit about expectations. This exercise helps partners uncover relationship rules, and aids in reducing misunderstandings, thereby improving overall communication and interaction.

1. Observe yourself and your partner, and use his help, if possible, to make the rules of your relationship explicit. What do you expect in relation to each other?

2. As you become more aware of your respective expectations, make a list of relationship rules. Add to the list whenever you think of or realize a new rule or expectation. Your partner can add to the list too.

3. Make the list accessible to both you and your partner, and refer to it when necessary.

TABLE 7.2 Relationship Rules

Expectations	Specific rule
Greeting when entering or leaving home	Say "Hi" when coming home or "See you later" when leaving.
Offering help with packages	When I come home with packages, ask if I need help with them.
Help around the house	Look at the chore list every day and do the chore listed. Ask if you can do more.

Some of these expectations may seem like common sense to you but may not come naturally to your partner. Whenever possible, be explicit about your expectations in order to help your partner know what you expect and give her the best chance of coming through for you.

Constructive Criticism

There are times when you need to approach a delicate topic with your partner, such as poor grooming or uncomfortable social behavior. Many people with AS can be very sensitive to personal critique. Being used to correction and criticism, they can become critical of themselves and others. Black-and-white thinking can lead them to feel worthless for being imperfect. Your partner can experience your concern or disagreement as negative judgment and rejection, so his reaction may be to turn these feelings back on you.

Sometimes people with Asperger's syndrome become defensive or withdraw when confronted with seemingly small requests or criticisms. To avoid your partner's defensiveness, be careful not to make unreasonable assumptions about her behavior or motivations. You do need to express your feelings, but it helps to do so in a way that doesn't leave your partner feeling attacked or harshly judged. Approaching your partner in a positive way, at a neutral time, when she is relaxed, can help her to feel more open to receiving constructive feedback or new ideas.

Be as authentic and factual as possible, so that your partner can make sense of your feedback. Instead of offering negative observations that your partner could interpret as a personal attack, offer feedback with a goal toward improvement; show your partner that he can improve something by making a change. Instead of just voicing concerns or problems, try offering a solution. Model how you want your partner to deal with criticism, even though it may be hard to listen when your partner criticizes you. Listen actively to what your partner says. He may take your feedback better if criticism flows constructively between you as the norm in your relationship.

More Ways to Offer Constructive Feedback

* Try to put yourself in your partner's place and understand how your feedback might affect her.

* Offer feedback about changeable behaviors, not his natural traits or character.

* Start by describing the behavior you see or experience.

* Focus on a specific situation rather than general behavior.

* Be open to dialog with your partner, rather than making accusatory assumptions.

* Do not compete against your partner; compete with your partner against a problem or issue.

* Offer feedback in a way that allows your partner to make her own decisions about what should be done; this makes it more likely that she'll follow through.

* Deal with one topic at a time: don't trump up charges or throw the book at your partner. Too many demands at once will be hard to understand and difficult to fulfill.

These ideas should give you a good head start in raising certain issues with your partner. As always, remember that you, your partner, and your partnership are each unique. Experiment with your own ways of handling things to come up with the combination of factors that works best for the two of you

Improving Communication

To continue improving your relationship communication, consistently use the rules for making discussions productive, along with the tips for asking for what you need and active listening. Keep the suggestions for providing constructive feedback and resolving arguments in mind whenever you let your partner know the things that bother or upset you and that you both need to work on. In addition, the following tips may be helpful in developing communication that works.

* Offer detailed, precise instructions, but keep them as brief as possible; provide only the necessary information.

* Give specific verbal or written requests (not implied or suggested ideas).

* Allow for time-outs and emotional space when needed and without criticism. Make sure to set a time frame for returning to the discussion to avoid building resentment.

* Be patient but persistent. Give your partner time to think about and respond to your concerns.

* Use "I" statements. State how you feel, and avoid blaming your partner. Rather than "You never do a thorough job; once again, you didn't sweep under the desk," try "I get upset when I see dust bunnies lying under my desk." Taking responsibility for your own reactions helps make your conversations more positive and useful.

* Stay calm. Keep discussions at a typical conversational volume. Take a deep breath and compromise.

These ways of interacting and communicating need practice. However, changes made in your relationship as a result of them can have an increasingly beneficial effect for you and your partner. The more you both pay attention to each other when communicating your ideas, feelings, and needs, the more you both will feel taken care of and want to do more of the same for each other. No matter the specific topic of discussion, find positive things to say about your partner and be respectful. Bring up emotional issues at a quiet, neutral time, if possible, so that you can speak calmly and your partner can focus and listen.

EXERCISE 7.3 Make Discussions Productive

Sometimes couples need rules to follow to help make their conversations, especially about heated topics, more productive. This exercise helps you to develop conversational rules.

1. Use the general tips for communicating as a starting point. Work with your partner to establish rules that you both agree to follow during potentially heated discussions.

2. Try a few discussions where you attempt to follow these rules.

3. Review the rules that worked for you and the ones that didn't.

4.   Revise your rules to fit your relationship reality.

5.   Make this into a "contract," and sign it along with your partner.

Most partners will at least give this a try, although if your partner refuses, you can establish your own list to abide by. You may not see immediate results, but be flexible and keep trying. Your changing attitude and behavior might help encourage your partner to feel less negativity and help soften his inflexible positions.

Misunderstandings

Unless you communicate clearly and directly, your partner may find your needs and interactions confusing. She may realize that you hold certain expectations of her, but may have trouble figuring them out. Your partner's uncertainty can lead to anxiety even within the very relationship that was supposedly formed to be a safe haven from the harshness of the outside world.

Nuances of verbal communication affect your relationship communication. Sometimes you might think that your tone of voice or your sarcastic words make your feelings clear to your partner. But your partner may not pick up parts of your communication, such as tone or sarcasm, resulting in miscommunication. One non-AS partner I see, Joan, left the room and walked into the kitchen when she had had enough of Ray's monologues on new archaeological findings. When she figured he had gotten the message, she returned, but he continued the conversation.

Rather than seething about unsatisfactory communication patterns, working to develop patterns that you feel good about will be worth the effort. "How can he not see this?" Joan asks in frustration. Our sessions help her understand that, of course, he can see her leaving the room, but he cannot read the meaning in her nonverbal behavior. She learned to tell him firmly but kindly when she had heard enough of a given topic. When the couple spends time talking at home alone, she listens to him for a while and then nicely says, "That's really interesting, Ray, but I need to switch to another topic now." When they are out with others, Ray knows to wrap up his monologue when Jan touches his shoulder with a firm but friendly squeeze.

Written Communication

Structuring some of your communication to your AS partner by using notes, charts, contracts, lists, and rules helps her to remember and complete tasks that she agrees to. Samples of these written forms of communication appear throughout this book as they pertain to specific areas you may need to work out with your partner. For many people with AS, written directions work best to make expectations clear. Written expectations also help your partner to remember what you want from her without your having to remind or nag.

WRITTEN REMINDERS

Some people with Asperger's syndrome enjoy writing and may write stories, poetry, love letters, or even books. Many struggle with writing but benefit from receiving written reminders and directions. Certain daily reminders, such as a "Don't forget your keys" note taped to the front door, may become invisible after a while, blending into the usual scenery. It helps when notes or lists are designed to be checked off, so that they don't become part of the home decor. Otherwise, you may need to move them, change them, or highlight them in some way so that your partner continues to notice.

TEXT MESSAGES AND E-MAILS

Technology helps many couples in which one partner has Asperger's to communicate in a way that sparks less emotional upset. Your partner with AS can also use text messages and e-mails during the day to let you know that he thinks about you.

In addition, you can use texts or e-mails to give your partner a heads-up about a change that might upset him. Phone calls and in-person notifications risk forcing you to deal with your partner's initial anger or upset reaction. If you call him to let him know that you'll be running an hour late and won't be home when he gets there, his initial reaction might be to get angry and yell. Similarly, if he walks in the door and finds that you haven't arrived home yet as he expected, he may get angry and withdraw for the evening. Even if you leave a note, his reaction may be to withdraw so that when you come home, you find him in his pajamas at the computer.

A text or e-mail gives your partner time to react and adjust before he gets home. He may return your text in all capital letters: "BUT YOU SAID YOU'D BE HOME BY 6?!" This is when you explain the situation without emotion in a brief text and even possibly ask him to start dinner. Chances are that by the time you come home at seven o'clock, exactly as he expected, he can be calm and have dinner in the oven. Of course, if you come home later than seven, you did not "keep your word," which may throw everything off. Even a text message as simple as "Burned dinner⊗; should we get pizza or Chinese?" can ease the initial confusion or betrayal of not getting "the usual" for dinner.

Your partner may need to be notified in advance about positive changes just as much as negative ones. One non-AS partner learned this the hard way. Pat's bicycle broke one morning, so her non-AS partner, Lee, drove her to the train station. Later, Lee decided that Pat would be very excited if she got to the train station and found her bike where she usually locked it and could ride home as always. So Lee had the bike fixed, brought it to the station, and left it for Pat to find when she got off the train after work. When Pat arrived at the station and saw the "broken" bike, she had a panic attack, and Lee received a very upset and angry call. Of course, once Lee explained that the bike was fixed, Pat was able to calm down and ride it home. A simple text message could have helped the situation and prevented the panic and meltdown: "Bike is fixed and waiting for you at the station☺."

Building Bridges

In one of the offices at our practice, a poster hangs with a picture of a bridge and a caption that reads, "Communication: Let's build bridges, not walls." Invariably, people with Asperger's make cynical comments, such as, "How neurotypical."

A recent article in *Psychology Today* (Helgoe 2010) debunks the myth that most people are outgoing and sociable. But being sociable and extroverted is usually considered better than being shy or introverted. The way neurotypical people often like to build bridges of communication starts with eye contact and social chitchat, which don't come naturally to people with AS. While social skills are important, we can relate to others using varying amounts of eye contact or chitchat. Understand that this may be as difficult for someone with Asperger's as it is for you to stay interested in an ongoing litany about weather patterns. Taking this pressure off can help your partner to develop these skills in his own way and at his own pace.

So, every time someone makes a comment, I realize that even in our office, where we promote neurodiversity as the norm, our poster can make some people feel unappreciated and perhaps judged by the views of the majority. But that represents only one interpretation, not the one we intend. We keep the poster because it still serves as a reminder to keep trying to build true bridges of understanding in all of our relationships, especially our intimate relationships.

Points to Keep in Mind

The way you and your partner communicate and interact sets the stage for feeling taken care of in your relationship or not. Your relationship expectations may include much more than you or your partner realized at the outset. Some people expect their AS partners to know how to act and relate simply by reading the cues. If your partner could learn what it means to be part of a couple simply by attending to unspoken rules of relationships (the hidden curriculum), she would know by now. Many people with AS lack the ability to pick up on important relationship and communication rules through subtle and unspoken cues and observations.

Too much pressure from you to relate or communicate in certain ways may become overwhelming, causing your partner to respond with anger, increased rigidity, or withdrawal. It may help to speak to your partner's rational, logical mind, instead of using emotional responses to get him to understand you and your needs. Focus on positive aspects of your relationship communication and work through the negative parts as best you can. You both need a positive attitude and respect to find a mutually agreeable balance between your world and his.

The tips presented for improving communication can work in your relationship with your AS partner. Ask for help if you need it; couples counseling can provide additional resources to resolve your tougher disagreements or communication difficulties. Your personal strengths in understanding and communicating may leave you feeling that you put in much more effort than your partner. But your effort will pay off as you both learn to manage your relationship interaction and communication in each other's world.

CHAPTER 8

An Emotional Connection

A good head and a good heart are always a formidable combination.

—Nelson Mandela

So how do you develop an emotional connection with someone with Asperger's syndrome? Your partner's primary struggles often have to do with forming and maintaining the one thing you may want the most. Your emotional connection may be unclear and static, or even feel nonexistent. Differences in the way you and your partner experience emotions may cause many areas of difficulty and misunderstanding.

Having Asperger's syndrome often makes it difficult to understand emotions—your own or someone else's—or to look at them from another perspective. The way you and your partner react and show emotions may be very confusing to each other. But you can still develop a strong emotional connection.

Some people with AS can be highly attuned to the emotional landscape around them. Others show very little emotion. Don't assume your partner doesn't possess emotions simply because she doesn't show them.

To complicate your emotional connection, Tony Attwood (1998) refers to the inability that some people with AS have in expressing appropriate emotions. They may laugh in circumstances where other people would show pain or sadness. Your partner may seemingly minimize your emotional issue, such as a death or potential job loss, by telling you, "Well, that's life," or "You hated working there anyway." Attwood stresses that practical, or even unusual, reactions do not define a person as cold or mentally ill. John Elder Robison (2007) wrote about this in *Look Me in the Eye: My Life with Asperger's*. He describes how he laughed on hearing of the death of someone, but not because he thought it was funny; in fact, he experienced great relief that it was not he or someone he knew well.

Emotional misunderstandings can gradually widen the distance between you and your partner, leaving you feeling separate and lonely. Forming or reforming those emotional connections can happen when you both learn to understand each other's reactions, readjust your expectations, and learn to relate in a way that's more likely to meet your emotional needs.

Emotional Deprivation

Do you sometimes feel alone, even when you're with your partner, or especially when you are with him? A significant amount of literature about relationships in which one partner has AS focuses on negative emotional effects for the neurotypical partner. Not getting your needs met can lead to negative consequences for both your mental and physical health. People remain in relationships that don't meet their needs for many reasons, and this cannot be blamed on Asperger's syndrome or your partner. There is much you can do to avoid feelings of emotional deprivation or to address them if they cause you to suffer.

Affective Deprivation Disorder

Maxine Aston (2009), a relationship counselor in the United Kingdom who specializes in helping couples in which at least one partner has AS, coined the term *Cassandra affective deprivation disorder*, also referred to as *affective deprivation disorder* (AfDD). This unofficial disorder refers to the emotional deprivation some neurotypical people attribute to years of living with someone with AS. Reported symptoms include anxiety, depression, low self-esteem, confusion, anger, depression, guilt, and loss of self. Theoretically, the problems can be compounded by friends and family who may believe that your partner is "just being a man," "too much of a feminist," or simply "just not that into you." The isolation and loneliness of experiencing your partner's limitations without outside support have been said to trigger and deepen the symptoms.

There is controversy concerning AfDD (which sounds professional but is currently not officially recognized). This disorder appears to blame problems in the relationship primarily on the partner with AS. It seems to ignore problems suffered by AS partners, who try hard to please the sometimes seemingly irrational (neurotypical) partner. Some partners with AS lament that they work hard to please their partners, but cannot change the core of their personalities. They then feel bad when they do not or cannot meet the neurotypical standard. The ultimate failure of relationships can lead many partners with AS to shut down and choose not to relate at all. This can also lead from frustration to anger and depression.

Feeling Alone

Mental health professionals understand that relationship problems between someone with AS and a neurotypical partner stem from issues on both sides. Shared responsibility and negative symptoms that affect both partners can be found at the core of such difficulties.

The depth of feelings on both sides of the partnership teaches us about both positions in these "mixed" relationships and how to help make them work. An important goal for you and your partner includes understanding feelings from both perspectives so that you can understand yourself, your partner, and your relationship more fully. It is important to come to a mutual understanding of each other and take responsibility for eliminating negative aspects of your life or relationship as you develop the life and love you strive for.

Ultimately, the responsibility for your own happiness begins with you. If you suffer poor emotional health, such as low self-esteem, confusion, anger, guilt, depression, anxiety, or poor physical health, please take action. Reach out for support from friends and family, see a doctor, contact a counselor, and do whatever it takes to feel good again. If you are living with feelings of serious emotional deprivation, you need to rethink your personal goals and possibly this relationship, which I will help you do in chapter 12. For now, work on developing a closer connection with your partner and getting your emotional needs met.

Emotional Exchanges

The idealized romance of books and movies promotes the common expectation that we know a partner's thoughts and desires without asking. But everyone in a real-life relationship knows the unrealistic expectation that we always know our partner's wishes. Through empathy, many people can often figure out others' thoughts or feelings relatively accurately. The more you get to know someone, the more it may be possible to make accurate predictions. People with AS often have challenges in this area.

Theory of Mind

Believing that your partner knows what you need and withholds it, rather than that she lacks understanding, can cause upset and confusion for both of you. Psychologists refer to *theory of mind* when discussing the knowledge people develop that what we think or experience is different from what others think and experience. People with Asperger's have a less-developed theory of mind than people without the syndrome (Baron-Cohen 2003). Your partner may find it difficult to understand that you have different emotional needs or opinions than she does. It may sound simple to you, but not to someone with AS.

Your ability to empathize with your partner helps you figure out what type of interaction might be needed with him in various situations. But the reverse may not be so. Your needs may be hard for your partner to understand, because Asperger's can make it difficult to see situations from another point of view. Your partner may be intelligent and articulate but still not understand your perspective. You may interpret your partner as self-centered when he goes on and on about his special interest without paying attention to your nonverbal cues, such as yawning or trying to move away. From his point of view, you encouraged elaboration when you asked a question.

Mutual Understanding

As someone with Asperger's syndrome, your partner has a perspective that develops rationally and logically. From a logical perspective, she would not be with you if she didn't want to share her life with you. This makes it seem unnecessary to have in-depth conversations about your relationship or to communicate love verbally; she already lives with you or spends time with you, which, to her, means the same thing.

According to non-AS "logic," if your partner loves and cares for you, then he will know what you feel, think, or want without your having to tell him. In waiting for him to demonstrate love your way, perhaps you miss his demonstration of deep connection because it appears so obvious and literal. You may not recognize your partner's attempts at making emotional connections, because he is likely to do this differently than you do. We explored ways to figure out what you want from your partner and how you can communicate this to him effectively. Make sure you tell your partner what you want him to know so you can be sure he knows it.

Understanding Feelings

Your partner may not have words for feelings and may not make a connection or distinction between physical sensations and emotional feelings. In a recent couple's session that became particularly tense and quiet, I asked the partners how they were feeling. The partner with AS responded, "My shoulder hurts." She made no connection between the tension in the room and the tension between her shoulder blades.

Feelings per se may not be all that important to your partner with AS. Many people with Asperger's syndrome lack the words for what they feel and have difficulty identifying feelings. You can, as one partner I know did, offer your partner a list of two hundred feeling words to choose from so that he can share his feelings with you each day. In this particular couple, this helped so much that the AS partner finally shared his feelings! Each day he would read the list of feelings and identify at least one or two of them to share. His partner felt very glad about this, but only temporarily, because several months later, he still read from the list each day.

When the couple came to me, the partner with AS said, "She wants me to be able to share my feelings without the list, and the only way I can do that is if I memorize the list. Should I do that?" While not a typical act of love, this was an offer of love on his part nonetheless. Many AS partners "pretend to be normal" by, in fact, memorizing such lists. Their efforts to perform these acts only so that they can get along better with neurotypical partners often go unrecognized and unappreciated.

It's not a bad idea to understand that your partner may need a list of words to choose from to talk to you about his feelings, and he may do so if you ask him to. This might help you come to understand your partner and strengthen your connection. But it may not be necessary to promote his own sense of connection. Would you memorize a list of two hundred historical dates or mathematical equations if it let your partner know that you love him?

Of course, your partner doesn't want you to feel bad, especially about her. But knowing that you do, without knowing what to do about it, causes frustration. Your partner also wants to avoid negativity coming her way in the form of your upset or disappointment in her. She most likely wants to please you and may not quite know what would do it. It will help to learn to translate feelings into specific desires or needs that your partner can actually perform or take care of for you in some way.

Some people complain initially that having to work at give-and-take takes away the good feeling of being truly cared for: "If he cared about me, I wouldn't have to teach him how to shut up about his own interests and listen to mine." Your partner does care and wants to show you that he does. That's why he may try to do this for you even though it's difficult and does not come naturally.

Getting Emotional Needs Met

Empathizing with others and understanding their needs makes most people feel connected and cared for. In general, neurotypical people understand another person's perspective better than someone with AS, but they also use this skill to make inaccurate assumptions. For example, many people like a nice, warm hug when they are upset, but many do not. People who prefer hugs tend to offer a hug for comfort, whether or not it actually comforts the other person. This exposes a blind spot in human understanding. It takes even deeper compassion to step outside your own understanding and truly give others what they want and need, not what you would want and need in the same situation.

Your partner may be very connected to you, although you may not feel it or recognize her attempts to show you. You may need to make your desires more explicit than you would like, but if you don't make your needs perfectly clear, your partner may not understand them.

Feeling More Connected

Using logic can help you to relate better to your partner and help him understand you. You may express sadness and hurt feelings for years without your partner showing an understanding of how sad or hurt his behavior makes you feel. To someone with AS, such feelings may seem confusing or irrational, because feelings tend to change and do not follow an objective, rational pattern. After years of hearing your explanations, your partner may understand that he lets you down in some very important ways but may not really comprehend that the emotional connection you crave is lacking in your relationship.

Your partner can learn to do certain things to ensure that you feel connected. Small acts that may seem unimportant to him, such as responding to your tears by handing you a tissue and sitting with you, can be easy to learn and can offer you a sense that he cares. In all likelihood, your partner does care, and therefore learning this will be worthwhile for both of you. Sometimes partners complain, "If he has to learn this, then he doesn't really love me." But the truth is that it probably has nothing to do with your partner's love for you. Your partner just may not feel the need to love and be loved in the same ways that you do. But because your partner loves you, he will work hard to learn what it takes to help you feel it. So, as he sits there and hands you a tissue, he feels love—not because he handed you a tissue but because you seem calmer and content now, and that feels good to both of you.

Most partners are willing to do little things to help you feel loved and connected if they know specifically what makes you feel that way. You can ask for things such as:

* Verbal expressions of love and interest

* A phone call or e-mail during the day

* Cards, flowers, or notes

Sending you text messages to touch base and connect with you during the day may make no rational sense to your partner, unless you translate this action into a rational need or idea. Try appealing to his sense of logic; help him understand the tasks necessary for the smooth operation of your relationship system.

EXERCISE 8.1
Developing Your Relationship Connection

Through this exercise both you and your partner can gain some clear ways to express and feel your relationship connection.

1. Use at least five slips of paper or 3 by 5 index cards to write things you do that help you to feel connected to your partner.

2. Use additional slips of paper or cards to write at least five things you would like your partner to do that would help you feel connected to her. For example, you may need (and get) things like greetings on arrivals and departures, compliments, sitting or walking together, and e-mails.

3. Have your partner make a list of things she does to help her feel connected to you and things she may need from you to feel connected or good around you.

4. Share each other's cards and discuss the various ways each of you currently connect and how you would like to connect in the future.

Highlight the things that you would like each other to do to help you feel more connected or loved.

5. Put the cards in two jars or shoe boxes, using one box for the things you want your partner to continue or begin to do and one box for the things she wants you to continue or begin to do.

6. Each of you can pick an item out of your shoe box so that you are doing at least a few small things for one another each week. Making a rule to do a certain number of these things automatically each week can help with the common perception that the relationship feels too rigid and lacks spontaneity. When incorporating one or two items a week seems easy, you can increase the frequency of doing loving acts until you get as close to each other's ideal as possible. Believe it or not, too much loving is possible, so stick to your partner's ideal and be open to change as necessary.

7. Actions that make you feel loved and the necessary frequency of taking these actions can change for either one of you. Review the lists periodically to ensure that you continue on the same wavelength as your partner. If your partner doesn't want to fill out cards, you can still discuss ways of connecting and offer her a list of ways to increase your feeling of connection. Make sure to ask your partner about things she would like you to do for her that would help her to feel good in relation to you.

Feeling Disconnected

Your needs and those of your partner may be too different for you to meet each other's needs as much as you both want. This doesn't mean that your partner can't change or do anything to help improve your relationship. There remains much that you both can do for each other. Realizing that the problem stems from differences between your respective emotional and physical resources and needs can be a first step. In all likelihood your partner doesn't mean to intentionally hurt or reject you, and may feel sad about your interpretation of his behavior.

CONNECTING WITH OTHERS

It is important to pursue your own interests and develop a life that you enjoy living. You can enjoy living with your partner without doing everything together. The following ideas can help you to feel more balanced and to be less dependent on your partner.

* Seek support from support groups, either online or locally, that understand and focus on issues relevant to partners of people with AS.

* Reach out to family, friends, or a professional for support. Some people find their spiritual or religious group helpful.

* Exercise: walk, run, dance, or go to the gym.

* Go out with friends; enjoy activities with them that your partner doesn't appreciate.

* Find a creative pastime that you truly enjoy.

* Pamper yourself with a massage, a manicure, or a new sweater.

* Write in your journal.

It can feel empowering and invigorating to go out on your own and connect with others. Coming home to your partner after enjoying time on your own can make your reunion more interesting and energizing for both of you. Your increased independence may help your partner with AS to feel less relationship pressure and may give her more energy for you.

Loneliness and Solitude

For many people with Asperger's syndrome, solitude offers the best way to recharge emotional resources. People with AS can be content for long periods alone. A problem may arise when you interpret your partner's need to be alone as a relationship communication. The message people with Asperger's give out when they need to be alone is that they feel overwhelmed and need time to recharge mentally and emotionally.

But neurotypical partners commonly "read between the lines" and take withdrawal personally, causing many hurt feelings and arguments.

You can help your partner help you distinguish between when he needs time away from you due to anger or something between you, and when he needs to rest mentally by taking some time to be alone. You can develop a code word or expression, such as, "I really need my quietude," for your partner to let you know when he needs solitude and when he feels ready to relate to you again. You can trust what he says about this; he is unlikely to change the truth to make you feel better.

Many outgoing or more socially oriented people try to fix their partners' enjoyment of being alone. Your partner doesn't need to be fixed in her preference for solitude any more than someone else needs to be cured of a preference for social activity. Social skill and the ability to deal with people in various situations is very important. But periods of solitude offer one way that people with AS relax and recharge.

Relating to others can be so exhausting that one couple reached an agreement whereby, when the AS partner wants a break from the living-room conversation with friends, he can reach into a nearby drawer, where they keep a physics textbook that he enjoys reading and that relaxes him. Their friends understand that he needs to do this from time to time, and know not to take it personally. This way he doesn't have to leave the room; his friends love his company—quirks and all. Most partners would not agree to such an extreme arrangement, but it works for this couple. You can find ways to respect your partner's need for solitude and allow him to recover without the added stress of your criticism and upset.

One way to lessen your feelings of rejection or abandonment during these times is to make a list of things you want your partner to do that communicate love, even during periods of alone time. This list obviously should not include things like spending time together in any way, or other contact that interferes with her emotional need for solitude. But your partner may be able to do small things that help you to feel connected even as she takes care of herself. Sample items to put on your list may include things like sending a short text message to let you know she's thinking of you, or stopping on her way home to pick up your favorite Chinese food. Offering nonjudgmental support of your partner's needs will help her to offer the same to you in return.

Points to Keep in Mind

The neurological wiring of people with Asperger's syndrome can make it difficult for your partner to understand emotional give-and-take. Responding to your emotional needs can be problematic, because your partner may not understand your needs or how to meet them—even if you've told him many times. He may experience emotions intellectually, and struggle to respond to his own needs. Your partner's emotional responses may sometimes sound cold and formal rather than loving. He may understand emotions logically rather than feel them the way that you do, and this can lead to misunderstanding.

Trying to develop the type of emotional connection that someone without AS requires may overwhelm your partner at times, causing a good bit of stress within and between you. At the same time, it would be unfair for your partner to use having AS as a reason to never step outside her comfort zone, when it really means a lot to you. Feelings, both yours and your partner's, must be understood from the perspective of the person who feels them. Feelings do not need to be right or wrong; if we feel something, we feel it, and feelings need attention.

It may be very difficult for your partner to meet your emotional needs, but don't allow his limitations to lead you into a state of deprivation. You or your partner may need to view your own and each other's feelings from a new perspective in order to understand their value and purpose in helping to strengthen your connection and develop intimacy.

CHAPTER 9

Sex and Intimacy

There are two ways to reach me: by way of kisses or by way of the imagination. But there is a hierarchy: the kisses alone don't work.

—Anaïs Nin

Couples in which one partner has Asperger's syndrome can enjoy a gratifying sexual relationship. According to Canadian psychologist Isabelle Hénault (2006), people with Asperger's demonstrate the same sexual interests, issues, and diversity as people in the general population. Adults with AS appear interested in sex to various levels and degrees, just like everybody else.

Many non-AS adults need the feeling of connection and intimacy in order to have a positive sexual relationship. An emotional connection is important for many adults to develop intimacy. Tending to emotional and physical intimacy may not constitute part of your partner's natural focus, leaving you feeling as if she doesn't care about or love you. Sometimes sexual needs may be met but not intimacy needs, and sometimes when sex depends on intimacy, none of these needs get met. This, too, can change.

Developing an Intimate Connection

Intimate communication involves sharing emotions and intimate thoughts, along with many nonverbal signals and cues. Partners with Asperger's syndrome may be uncomfortable with the type of intimate communication that non-AS partners need for an intimate connection.

Non-AS partners who initiate couples therapy because of problems in this area often desire more intimacy in their overall relationships, in addition to greater frequency of sexual relations. They want their partners to spend more time with them, to sit with them in the evening and talk about their day. They want their partners to learn to touch them in ways that they enjoy and that please them. They want their partners to listen and pay attention to what makes them feel good, and how they want to be treated before, during, and after lovemaking.

Romance

Maybe your partner seemed very romantic in the beginning. This is often true, especially of certain people with AS, who seem to have a more natural ability than other people with AS to understand emotions. Previous experiences and understanding of social relationships also make a difference in intimacy and sexuality for someone with AS. Learning about relationships from books, movies, and TV shows may help as well. Jason learned how to be romantic through songs. But this might not result in an adult who understands how to be intimate in the long run. Most neurotypical partners expect romance to not only continue but also give way to deeper intimacy.

Intimacy

Intimacy refers to more than just physical intimacy, and physical intimacy refers to more than just sex. In addition, sex in an intimate relationship does not grow only from physical intimacy; many people also need an emotional connection for sex to be most enjoyable. Intimacy involves sharing hopes, beliefs, dreams, physical affection, and sex. While sex is important to relationship intimacy, it is not the only part of it.

Every couple develops their own ideas about what intimacy means for them. These ideas come from both partners; they are a part of the shared reality that you two grow into as you get closer and your relationship grows. For some, intimacy involves walking hand in hand, sharing tea and conversation, or having sex. Because your AS partner may not have thought of defining intimacy before, her concept of it may be uncertain. She may be looking to you for guidance to help her understand the hidden curriculum in intimacy and your nonverbal cues for what you expect from her. This type of guidance may gradually help her move in the direction you hope for and not withdraw.

HOW ASPERGER'S MIGHT INTERFERE

Sex and intimacy can present major difficulties even for people without the complexities in relating that Asperger's adds to the mix. Adults with AS can have a delayed understanding of intimacy and sexual behavior. Characteristics of Asperger's syndrome that make understanding the rules of social relationships difficult will also affect your partner's ability to understand your intimacy and sexual needs.

Your partner's tendency to have a single focus, be inflexible, and need routine can affect your intimate and sexual relationship in many ways. Sometimes these traits can interfere with intimacy, such as when your partner spends so much time on the computer that it leaves no room for sex or intimate connection. Other times, the intimacy or the sex itself can pose difficulties by becoming the obsession or developing into a routine that cannot easily be changed.

As Tony Attwood (2007a) points out, the varying sensitivities of people with Asperger's syndrome can also affect their sexual activities. Too little sensitivity can cause problems in obtaining necessary stimulation for feeling full pleasure. Others with AS may be oversensitive to the experience of sex, or to particular types of touch or pressure on certain parts of the body. For example, your partner may not be able to relax and enjoy lying too close for very long.

Bodily odors can cause problems from both perspectives; for example, stale body odor can be very offensive to either partner, making it difficult to carry on in a sexual situation. Your partner may be absolutely unable to tolerate certain smells, touch, or sounds. By the same token, the right body lotion or music can help to enhance sex for you or your AS partner. It is also possible for people with AS who have certain sensitivities to become more comfortable with intimate touch.

Learning your partner's particular sensitivities and being entirely respectful of them is an important consideration. This may mean that there are certain parts of the body you cannot touch or certain types of touch you cannot use. Listen to your partner regarding his preferences; he may prefer touch to be firm, and may not be able to tolerate touch that is light or moving. Certain touch may be tolerable only at certain times or not at all. Touch that feels good to you may not feel good to your partner. Everyone is different in this regard.

Coping strategies will be different for every couple, depending on your needs and how they may and may not be met in your relationship. Be sure to make your expectations and desires as clear as possible and discuss them with your partner. Making rules and guidelines together for sex and intimacy will help to offset some of the ongoing issues you run up against.

Specific ideas to consider include introducing exploration or any needed changes gradually. Remember that these actions, too, will become routine unless your partner can tolerate constantly changing routine as part of your routine. Many people with AS tend to take rules seriously, which may cause problems in sexuality. Then again, if your partner thrives on rigid rules or schedules, try to get sex and intimacy on the schedule so that they become part of the routine.

Intimacy Needs

You may feel sad or resentful that your relationship lacks spontaneity or romance and that, once again, you have to be the one to plan or initiate any form of intimacy. At least, by doing this, you will make things happen in your relationship that have the potential to become new and more fulfilling patterns between you and your partner. Rather than leaving you feeling emotionally deprived, going for your intimacy needs can help bring you some of what you desire and help you to feel somewhat taken care of, rather than depleted.

EXERCISE 9.1   Increasing Intimacy

This exercise helps you to focus on the things you need more of in your relationship so that you can feel an increased intimate connection with your partner.

1.   Make a list of activities that you feel represent intimacy. Examples might include going for walks together; giving hugs; sending flowers; using specific verbal expressions, such as "I love you"; calling you during the day; or reading a book together.

2.   Discuss your list with your partner, and use her input to come up with things you can both do to increase the intimate connection between you. Help your partner understand the things you want and how she might best do them. Ask your partner for what you need in specific terms, such as a hug when she comes home each day. Perhaps she already does some things that you enjoy; make sure to offer appreciation and ask for her to continue doing them.

3.   Write the activities that you and your partner agree to do for each other on separate 3 by 5 index cards or slips of paper, and put a rubber band around them to keep them together.

4.   Make it a goal or a rule for you and your partner to randomly choose one statement or activity from the card pile to offer each other regularly. You can increase the frequency later, but for now start slowly. Focus on getting more of what you need without overwhelming your partner. New patterns usually need to be built slowly over time. Remember to do the things your partner wants from you too.

If you don't want to formalize this exercise, you can simply make a list and let your partner know what you want. If you do this, you may have to remind your partner every day that you want her to do something from your list. Some couples like to do this exercise using the cards because it separates the task from you a little bit and gives your partner responsibility for initiating intimacy. Given time, this can lead to some very nice, more inspiring routines.

A Satisfying Sexual Relationship

Over six months had passed since Jan and Blaise had enjoyed any sexual intimacy. Jan (the non-AS partner) asked, "Are we ever going to have sex again?" Blaise (the partner with AS) replied, "I'd like to think we will."

This brief exchange, once again, shows a difference in viewpoints: the non-AS partner expressing a desire or a hope and the AS partner thinking about it. Establishing an emotional connection with your partner goes beyond shared conversations and little things you do for each other. It also goes beyond thinking about it. While all of these factors are important in the intimacy process, most adults want to move deeper into physical intimacy.

In spite of their typical sexual interest, sex often does not drive adults with Asperger's syndrome in their quest to find a partner. This is frequently a very attractive quality that many non-AS women tell me factored into falling in love with an AS male. Your male partner with Asperger's syndrome was probably quite a gentleman when you first met. Many women appreciate the male who values and respects them as people, not sexual objects.

Physical Affection

Your partner with Asperger's may be very affectionate, or may not be comfortable offering or receiving physical affection at all. This apparent rejection can feel very bad to a non-AS partner but is not meant to reject you in any way. Your partner may have serious intolerance to certain types of touch, which may feel offensive, rather than sensual or enjoyable, for her. Work with your partner to figure out what kinds of touch can be tolerated. Sometimes knowing that a touch is coming helps your partner to get ready for it and tolerate it better. Not initiating physical affection typically has nothing to do with your AS partner's lack of affectionate feelings toward you.

SEX AND AFFECTION AS NONVERBAL COMMUNICATION

Sex and affection represent nonverbal communication that some adults with AS feel particularly successful with. Through a physical connection, they can show their love without getting tangled up in emotions and misunderstandings. The ability to offer love nonverbally helps some adults with Asperger's to be physically affectionate, which can be very positive for many couples. More often, it seems that adults with AS tend to show affection infrequently and at undesired levels of intensity; your partner may come on too strong or not come on at all.

Issues with the nonverbal aspect of sex and affection may also make it difficult for your partner with AS to navigate physical intimacy. The nonverbal cues that you send regarding whether or not you feel in the mood can be lost or misinterpreted. For your partner with AS, it may be very hard to tell the difference between your nonverbal cues for sex and your hints for affection. Because of your partner's tendency toward the practical, he may learn specific sexual techniques faster than he catches on to the "hidden sexual curriculum" of flirting and romantic gestures. If you work together, he can learn both.

Differences in Libido and Preferences

Among other things, desire for sex varies with timing, mood, energy level, and need for variety. Typical frequency of sexual relations in a couple can be more than once a day to once every few months or less. Each couple has to decide the quantity and quality that satisfies both partners.

Libido refers to your sexual energy or desire. Everybody has a different level of libido. Many people, some with AS, judge the success of a relationship on sexual frequency, because it is a concrete way to look at intimacy. The easiest sexual relationships, in terms of libido, occur when both partners have the same level of energy. If you and your partner both have a low libido, you probably won't have sex very often, but neither of you will be that concerned about it.

In the couples I see, it rarely works out this smoothly. More frequently, couples have to find a compromise that works for both partners. Often, that means that the lower-libido partner has to get in the mood a little more often than she prefers, and the higher-libido partner has to manage his sex drive so that all the pressure isn't on the other partner. In general, adults with AS seem to be more satisfied with a lower frequency of sexual activity than the general population (Hénault 2006), although more research is needed in this area.

Communicating about sexual preferences and libido involves speaking and listening—really listening—with the intent of solving problems in this area, just as with any other relationship problem. Focus on what both of you want to get from your sexual relationship and ways to make it more gratifying. You and your partner deserve a fulfilling life together; consider counseling if you cannot work things out as a couple.

EXERCISE 9.2   Improving Your Sexual Relationship

1.   Make three lists to share with your partner: one for what your partner does sexually that you like, one for things you would like your partner to do or try sexually, and, finally, one for things that you do not particularly enjoy. Be specific about what you hope for and include activities you wish for before, during, and after sex (for example, consider whether you want more or less foreplay; whether there are certain sexual positions you like or dislike; and whether you prefer to be held afterward, to talk for a while, or to fall right to sleep).

2.   Hopefully your partner will share similar thoughts with you and come up with her own lists so that you can also adapt to her sexual desires, preferences, and needs. Your partner may feel pressure to perform and may be uncomfortable with certain aspects of sex. As in other areas, if desires or needs are opposing, the two of you will have to work out compromises so that your sexual relationship can be pleasurable for both of you.

Pay attention to your sexual difficulties and do not allow sex to become a taboo subject in your relationship. Pick up a basic book about sex to help you be very clear about what you want or expect. Reading it together may be ideal, along with discussing and demonstrating how you both feel about various issues and ways of touching. If the topic remains too difficult for you and your partner to talk about, use the book to help you start the conversation, or seek help from a mental health counselor who can guide you through such discussions.

A gratifying sexual life is important in most intimate relationships. In *The Seven Principles for Making Marriage Work*, renowned relationship expert John Gottman asserts, "A major characteristic of couples who have a happy sex life is that they see lovemaking as an expression of intimacy, but they don't take any differences in their needs or desires personally" (Gottman and Silver 1999, 203). Although you can work alone to improve your own sexual responsiveness or sensitivity to your partner, your sexual and physical intimacy needs benefit most when you can discuss and work them out together. For this reason, sex is often the last area that comes together; couples often need to work out other relationship issues before they can adequately work together on sexual issues.

MASTURBATION

Masturbation is common and natural. Some people masturbate frequently, and some prefer not to engage in it at all. Masturbation can be a quick way to relieve stress or arousal without involving responsibility or the whole process of sex. Some partners masturbate when they are separated or ill, or to make up for some of the libido differences in their relationship. Masturbation can have a negative effect on your relationship if it takes the place of having sex together or if it damages anyone's self-esteem. Sometimes people feel that if your relationship were good enough, neither of you would feel the need to masturbate. Other couples enjoy masturbating together. Masturbation is okay as long as it doesn't interfere in any way with your relationship with your partner.

PORNOGRAPHY

For some couples pornography is fine, while for others, the use of pornography is a deal breaker. Many female partners consider pornography to be insulting, degrading, and a form of cheating; others may enjoy it. Many men seem to have less understanding about their partners' anger and do not see themselves as being unfaithful when they view porn. For someone with AS, masturbation and pornography can offer ways to satisfy arousal and relieve stress without the complicated sexual relationship that is usually involved in this process. Discovering your partner's pornography use may evoke many emotions, depending on your own views and feelings about it.

Some people do use pornography in unhealthy ways, viewing too much or becoming obsessive about it. This can create an obstacle to intimacy and sexual satisfaction in your relationship. If your partner with AS uses pornography too much, he may have learned that it was okay from other sources. If you are not okay with his level of involvement, he may need to hear from you. Your partner's pornography use may be considered harmful if he prefers viewing pornography over having sex with you; if it harms your relationship in any way; or if he denies using it in the face of evidence, refuses to discuss it, or lacks concern about your feelings on the issue.

Start by discussing this issue honestly and without judgment or accusation. Your partner may not have considered the effect of his use of pornography on you, and your conversation can help him to understand. Can you find a compromise, or is this a deal breaker for you? Keep an open mind, but be honest with your partner about what you can and cannot tolerate. Mistrust and anger about pornography can tear your relationship apart. Can your partner accept your compromise or lack of it?

AFFAIRS

Many adults with Asperger's syndrome, being rule bound, tend to stay within the primary relationship for sex and intimacy. In addition to following the known rules for monogamous relationships, which clearly discourage affairs, your AS partner has enough on her plate in trying to relate to and please you. I have met some adults with AS who appear somewhat naive and can be oblivious to flirtation, their own or someone else's. This area may need direct and specific communication to maintain the trust and boundaries of your intimate relationship. But your partner is probably not looking for more problems and yet another person to disappoint and change for.

Some of the non-AS partners who come to me for help reveal that they are considering having affairs to find what they lack in their relationships with their AS partners. They usually still love their partners but find the relationship intolerable, so they look for an escape as well as someone to offer the emotional connection they miss. Sometimes they hope that this, or even the threat of it, will mobilize the AS partner to fight for the relationship and become more affectionate and connected. It's more likely that your partner with AS will give up and withdraw even more from any emotional connection. If you want to connect with your AS partner, this strategy is not likely to serve your purpose. And, if you don't want to work on a connection with your partner, perhaps it's time to move on completely. Chapter 12 focuses on what to do when your relationship isn't working.

Trust

Both partners need to feel trust in order to feel close to each other. It's often hard for people with Asperger's syndrome to trust an intimate connection, because of years of misunderstanding and rejection. When they do come to trust you, the bond can be very strong. Your partner can feel shaken by any sense of disloyalty or lack of commitment. The movie *Adam* (Mayer 2009) tells the story of a young man with Asperger's in a relationship with the girl next door. At one point, Adam has a meltdown when he finds out that his girlfriend had known something but failed to tell him. This is such a huge breach of trust for him that it almost ends the relationship. Honesty in communication is paramount.

Points to Keep in Mind

You cannot assume that what you need and enjoy, in terms of an emotional connection, will be the same as what your partner enjoys. Many neurotypical adults are less likely to want sex when they feel unhappy or disconnected. Help your partner to understand how intimacy connects with sex for you. It may help to make specific, concrete goals to work on concerning having more emotional and sexual intimacy in your relationship. Learn your partner's likes and dislikes, and let him know yours clearly and explicitly. As with any other aspect of your relationship, if one of you feels unhappy, you both have a problem.

Intimacy may be another area that you need to take the lead with. For some adults with Asperger's syndrome, the quest for increased emotional and physical intimacy may be painstaking. In addition to your strength in relationships, you need tolerance, trust, good communication, and commitment. Your partner may need to learn to consider your requests and desires, just as you need to consider hers. This part of your system is one of the most unpredictable and hard to understand. Thus, it will be easier for you to navigate than it will be for your partner with AS.

At this point, you have worked through and thought about many of the most significant aspects of your relationship. Hopefully you found enough satisfaction or hope of attaining it that you keep compromising, working, and achieving a greater connection through continued communication and partnership. It takes time and energy to make intimacy and sex a priority in your relationship.

CHAPTER 10

Parenting Together

It is time for parents to teach young people early on that in diversity, there is beauty and there is strength.

—Maya Angelou

Many adults with Asperger's syndrome eventually want children. Because all aspects of raising children can't be covered here, this chapter deals primarily with challenges and solutions for issues that may arise in parenting with a partner who has AS. When couples come to me for guidance, I often stress that they must remember to work as members of the same team, not opponents. This holds true in parenting as in any other relationship area.

Some adults with Asperger's make great parents, while others have significant parenting challenges that stem from some of the core characteristics of AS. Parenting involves an intense emotional relationship between parent and child. Parents provide nurturance, discipline, guidance, care, and understanding, along with emotional and financial support. The fact that an adult can function well in other areas does not necessarily mean that he can be an effective parent.

Adding Kids

Adding kids is often an extension of your intimate relationship. The attention of non-AS partners usually shifts, with the baby or child becoming the primary focus of attention, at least initially. Non-AS partners often look to their co-parents to understand their depth of feeling for the child and their interest in the child's growth and development. For parents with AS, this may not happen, because their own thoughts and needs may continue to dominate their focus.

The new responsibility of both parents for the life of a totally dependent child may highlight some of the difficulties in your different perceptions. As with other aspects of relationship responsibility, the non-AS partner often takes on most of the parenting duties. The partner with AS may appear less capable because of some of her relative weaknesses, such as difficulty understanding a baby's nonverbal cues, or not being clear about what her role and responsibilities should specifically entail.

Once you add children to your household, the inequality in responsibility can get raised to new heights. Patterns that develop tend to be very difficult to change. If possible, involve your partner from pregnancy onward by talking about expectations, reading parenting manuals together, and generally preparing for the birth. From the beginning, do not let things slip, because they may become harder to change once they become rigid routines.

Mothers with Asperger's

If the mom is the one with Asperger's syndrome, she may experience even more pressure than a male partner with AS to handle the family's social and emotional life. Mothers with AS whom I know must often work extra hard at understanding some of the issues that typical mothers seem to intuit naturally. Mothers and fathers with AS can both experience a lot of trouble understanding their children, but the mothers often seem to show greater understanding and empathy. Both usually love their children and try hard to overcome weak areas to give their children the best parenting they can.

Raising Children

Children don't come with directions. As with other relationship behaviors, we learn parenting from our own experiences, as well as from TV, books, and movies. Such role models can affect the type of parental roles partners adopt and the way they work together to raise the children. Some people seem to have more natural ability to take care of children than others.

How Asperger's Can Make Parenting Difficult

Many difficulties may arise for parents with AS in raising children. Some adults with Asperger's syndrome have a hard time interacting with and relating to children. Parents must often rely on reading their children's faces to understand and respond to emotions such as joy, fear, distress, sleepiness, and sadness. Most parents, especially mothers, are often highly attuned to signals from their children. Your partner with AS may seem distant, quiet, or unemotional with the kids. One divorced parent in my practice simply has no need or desire to spend more time with her kids than the contracted dinner out once a week. For others, the children may add too much chaos and lead to increased emotional meltdowns.

Anxiety or heightened sensitivities may make the unpredictable, disruptive, changeable, demanding, noisy, messy world of the child very difficult to cope with. Children have minds of their own, and life with them often defies even the best planning. Neurotypical partners sometimes feel that the partner with AS acts like a child and cannot be relied on as a co-parent. Some non-AS adults avoid leaving their partners in charge or responsible for the children. Sometimes concern is warranted, although, often, the parent with AS resents this for valid reasons.

EMPATHY IN CHILD REARING

Parents with Asperger's syndrome may not be intuitive about the thoughts, wishes, knowledge, or intentions of their own children. This can be especially important when dealing with an infant. One very upset mom explained to me that while her AS partner was holding the baby, the baby babbled, "B-b-b," and pointed at the desk in the room. The mother was very upset that the baby's father didn't realize from the baby's increasingly frantic behavior that he wanted the bottle that was sitting on the desk. When we discussed this situation with the dad, he honestly did not understand how it was obvious that the baby wanted the bottle, when the baby babbles often and points all the time too. How was he supposed to know that this time, the baby really wanted something?

Many parents instinctively let their children win at games and gradually offer them losses until they can handle a real competition. In this scenario, parents help their children learn to be good at both winning and losing. At least one AS father I see in my practice did not know this instinctively. He felt that as the man of the house, he had to win or he would lose respect. When he played games with his kids, he had to win every time, or he got angry and refused to play. Either way, his games with the children ended with the children in tears and their mother beside herself with frustration at her husband's "childlike" behavior.

Some parents with AS react strongly to misperceived behavior of the children. Such misperceptions are related to theory of mind (see chapter 8), because some parents with AS can have difficulty distinguishing between intentional and accidental actions of children. One AS father I spoke with complained that the children totally destroyed order in the kitchen and wreaked havoc with food storage. His partner described an incident in which they both came home from grocery shopping and asked their ten-year-old child to put the food away. About an hour later, the dad went into the kitchen to start dinner and bellowed into the next room, "What idiot put the cans of soup on the shelves in random order?" The father's obvious disappointment and anger hurt the child. The mother was furious that her partner criticized the child for being imperfect when she felt he deserved kudos for helping.

FOCUS AND DISTRACTIBILITY

People with AS may have difficulty focusing their attention, especially if something is already absorbing them. They sometimes get so overfocused on an area that changing their focus seems unlikely. Sara let me know that when her partner Ian focuses on something, such as his work on the computer, she fears that the house could literally burn down and he would not notice. This can be an area that needs special attention to ensure everyone's safety when the parent with AS stays alone with the children.

SENSORY VIOLATIONS

Related to problems of attention and distractibility, your partner with Asperger's syndrome may become neurologically overwhelmed in certain child-friendly settings. Your partner may find playing with your child at the neighborhood playground to be much more manageable than a day at a theme park. Parents with AS cope with overwhelming sensory violations by leaving the situation, shutting down, or melting down. Loud noises or confusing commotion can make it hard for such parents to be there with their children. Energy depletion can also be a problem. By the end of the workday, many parents with AS have little energy or resources left to deal with their children.

Co-parenting

Rigidity in routine, sensory issues, anxiety, and underdeveloped theory of mind are issues that may affect your partner's ability to parent at times. Many coping strategies for parenting are available, depending on the specific parenting strengths that you and your partner possess. For example, if your partner has difficulty understanding the baby's nonverbal cues, consider teaching her three things to try when the baby cries: pick him up, change his diaper, or give him a bottle. If this parent must be left alone with the child, make sure there is someone to call for backup, just in case. You can also write down other suggestions about how to proceed, such as playing with the baby gym or playing peekaboo.

As your child grows, you can teach her to verbalize her needs and intentions to make herself more clearly understood. You can also teach your partner rules, such as that children need to learn how to win and lose, and that parents are responsible for helping them to do this by modeling good sportsmanship.

Many people with AS tend to say what they think, honestly and without much hesitation. It can be difficult to keep an AS dad from commenting that his daughter should not have one more cookie because she already weighs too much, or from telling his son that he looked like a fool when he made that big play and fumbled. Both parents need to develop and agree on general rules that specifically include topics that shouldn't be discussed with the children, such as criticizing their weight or putting down their abilities. A specific list of ways to offer loving and helpful feedback can also help your partner to learn to relate more positively to the children.

Parenting Rules

Problems with child rearing are often the result of rules, even ones that seem obvious to you, not being made explicit to your partner. Just as you made a list of rules regarding your relationship, you need to spell out parenting rules, including the behaviors that will and will not be tolerated. The sample rules suggested next stem from some of the previous examples and show how you can use incidents in your family to make your own rules. In addition, you need to negotiate house rules for the benefit of everyone living in the house. If you or your partner with AS has certain needs that can be spelled out in rules for everyone to follow, the household may run more smoothly. Making a list of rules will give you a starting point for current and future parenting decisions.

Sample Parenting Rules

*   *Rule 1:* No name-calling; this includes not referring to an "anonymous" person by a negative name if you have reason to believe that person is a member of the household (as in, "What idiot did this?").

* *Rule 2:* If you have a system for doing things that must be done a certain way, teach it to your family members. If others have trouble following your system, you may have to do the tasks yourself or make compromises.

* *Rule 3:* If you ask a family member to do something for you and the person does it, offer praise for the effort, even if the task was not performed perfectly.

Parenting Goals

Your goals related to household organization and decision making may also help you both to work as a team to parent your children. Your own personal goals can include things like speaking calmly to your partner in front of the children or purposely speaking well of your partner so that your children see your respect for their other parent. You and your partner can also develop partnership goals for parenting together.

Making specific parenting goals concerning who will do what and when helps your family system run more efficiently and also encourages closer bonds among all of you. It may be helpful to review chapter 5 if you need help to develop parenting goals for your partnership. Chapter 13 includes a sample relationship agreement that can certainly be adapted to parenting. If you and your partner continue to have difficulty negotiating rules and boundaries together, you may need help from a third party, such as a mental health professional.

Clarify Responsibities

Work together as a team with your partner to clarify parenting responsibilities, including specific duties. Most couples have different parenting styles, and you can expect this to be true for you and your partner. Even when you disagree with the way your partner handles a situation, you can work as a teammate by supporting your partner in front of the children. When you two are alone, you can discuss the situation and agree on how to handle it the next time.

You can make parenting responsibilities for you and your AS partner explicit in various ways. One way involves sitting with your partner and brainstorming about all of the child-care duties that you can think of. Don't worry if you miss some; you can always add more later. Decide who will carry out each responsibility and how often or when each task gets done. A sample parenting checklist looks like this:

Sample Parenting Checklist

Responsibility	Who will do it	Circle on completion
Walk to bus	Jaz	M T W R F
Make lunch	Ron	M T W R F
Help with homework (English)	Jaz	M T W R F
Help with homework (math, history), as needed	Ron	M T W R F
Bath time	Jaz	M T W R F
Bedtime story	Jaz	M T W R F
Instrument practice	Ron	M T W R F

In this chart, the letters stand for the days of the week; R stands for Thursday. You and your partner can come up with your own codes, as long as you both agree on and understand them. Focus on your partner's strengths and assign jobs that he can legitimately do, so that this won't be a setup for failure. Rather than make a list that shows your name thirty times and your partner's name twice, put just a few of your own duties down. This way you both work off of the checklist, but you personally do not have to work off of the checklist for everything you do. Perhaps there's another area of responsibility where your partner will carry more of the weight, such as taking care of the garden, the car, or all of your high-tech equipment (TV, computer, CD and DVD players).

In addition, surely you can find areas where your partner is good with the children, if not responsible for them. Does she make them laugh, and does she play with them? Does she show them "cool" things, like the slugs under rocks and the way the water flows in the streets around the sewers? Does she use funny voices when she reads to them, and help them understand or care for your pets?

EXERCISE 10.1   Focus on Strengths

This exercise highlights the parenting strengths of your AS partner and helps you to focus on getting more help from him by appreciating his positive parenting skills.

1.   Brainstorm about the positive parenting skills that your partner possesses.

2.   Write a compliment to your partner about his parenting skills, fold it, and place it in a jar or bowl.

3.   For every three compliments you put in the jar, you can put one slip with a need for improvement. Make the items that need improvement something specific that your partner can actually do.

4.   Have your partner read one slip of paper each day and either bask in the compliment or receive a suggestion for improvement, such as "Please let Johnny know that you're proud of him today." Maybe you can offer a few different ways to say this so your partner can learn positive scripts to help him with this one. Once your partner improves certain skills, you can trade for other ones, as long as there is always a ratio of three to one in the jar.

Remember to let your partner show appreciation for your parenting strengths in this way as well. You can both do this for other areas of your relationship too.

Telling the Kids about Asperger's Syndrome

One non-AS father tries to take over all responsibility (resentfully) for the family. He shields his children from their mother's apparent lack of mothering skills and her occasional meltdowns. A healthier way to relate as a family involves helping the children understand that different people have different strengths and that the children bear no responsibility for their mother's meltdowns.

Children are resilient and can handle different rules and types of parenting. Kids usually learn to love and accept who their parents are. They are capable of learning to be sensitive and tolerant. They can understand that issues causing their parents stress are not their fault and can be avoided, as with the family with a parent who is allergic to nuts or pets, or who has diabetes. For many families, if, when, and how the children should be told about their AS parent creates a difficult dilemma. You may need outside support to help you figure out the best way to manage this for your family.

Children learn about intimacy in their family of origin. The purpose of telling the children that a parent has AS is not to make them responsible for that parent but to validate the children's feelings. Children are intuitive and perceptive. Sometimes I work with families in which the parents express concerns about letting the children know that one of them has Asperger's. When I meet privately with the children, they sometimes express that their AS parent is different but they don't want to bring this up in front of their parents. Thus, the parents and the children share a similar secret, and neither wants to burden the other with it.

Children may need help to understand the sometimes-confusing behavior of the AS parent, which can be misinterpreted negatively as the children's fault or as rejection. In explaining their own behavior, AS parents should not rely too much on young children for patience or guidance. But they can be honest, for example, when they are in a restaurant that is just too loud or too bright.

Sometimes children need counseling around some of the behaviors they grow up with related to a parent with AS. Validating the experience of your children aids in their healthy adjustment. In addition, what better way to teach your children empathy and tolerance than to begin with the members of your own household?

Rising to the Challenge

In general, most parents with Asperger's syndrome can get beyond their own weaknesses and use their strengths to act in the best interests of their children. Raising kids can be a very difficult challenge but also a great opportunity. In *Grown-Up Marriage: What We Know, Wish We Had Known, and Still Need to Know about Being Married*, Judith Viorst (2003, 84) states, "[W]hile parenthood makes parents short on sleep and very long on emotional deprivation, and gives them new things to bicker and battle about, it is also, or can be, a chance for a husband and wife to develop some admirable new qualities."

Statistically, having Asperger's syndrome increases the likelihood of having a child with AS or AS-like symptoms. Many parents with AS have children with profiles similar to their own who can be a challenge to parent, especially for the non-AS partner. When it comes to these kids, it is often the parent with Asperger's who can relate the most and understand the child and her development, because it reflects his own. The parent with AS can sometimes be most helpful in understanding and helping a child with AS to learn and cope with expectations.

Points to Keep in Mind

Many parents with Asperger's syndrome are eager to parent according to their children's best interests, and they work hard to understand them. You and your partner must honestly assess whether the responsibility of children presents too much of a challenge for your partner or if she just falls short of your standard of care. If a true safety issue exists, then you really do need another plan for taking care of the children. But if you are just annoyed at the different way your partner cares for the kids—you don't like what she feeds them or what she lets them watch on TV—you have to take a step back and allow her to be different from you.

If it comes to an issue of deep values, you must come to some form of agreement with your partner. Ranting and raving will not help your partner to change his parenting skills. Instead, work to find areas of strength that your partner can offer in helping to raise the children. Can he help out with science and math homework? Take the child out to buy the proper materials for her school project? Maybe they can enjoy playing music together, or your child can learn to help with the jobs around the house that your partner excels at.

Most parents feel tired by the end of the day. A parent with AS may literally have nothing left to give by the time bedtime rolls around. Be realistic about your partner's strengths and weaknesses. As always, highlight the strengths, downplay the weaknesses, and work together as a team.

CHAPTER 11

Co-existing Conditions

Nothing ever exists entirely alone;
everything is in relation to everything else.

—Buddha

Mental health problems are very common. A major study estimates that about half of the general population in the United States will experience significant mental health symptoms at some point in their lifetimes (Kessler et al. 2005). Differences in the brain appear to leave people with Asperger's syndrome susceptible to various accompanying conditions. Many professionals notice overlapping conditions in almost all people with autism. This chapter focuses on the specific overlapping conditions that may also affect your relationship.

Conditions Associated with Asperger's Syndrome

Symptoms of anxiety, depression, obsessive-compulsive disorder, bipolar disorder, attention deficit disorder, and other conditions often go hand in hand with autism spectrum conditions, including Asperger's syndrome. Issues such as anxiety and depression may even develop or worsen specifically as a result of challenges presented by AS.

Mental health conditions involve both physical and psychological symptoms, and often require treatment, otherwise symptoms tend to get worse. The most effective treatment sometimes involves a combination of medication and psychotherapy to help manage difficult symptoms. Natural remedies, such as herbs, teas, and vitamin supplements, may also be helpful in reducing certain symptoms.

Before we explore some of the most common conditions that people with AS tend to struggle with and how they may affect your relationship, I'll offer some general guidelines for helping your partner cope while also taking care of yourself. If your partner shows signs of any of the conditions discussed in this chapter, consider consulting an appropriate medical or mental health professional. Many people feel more comfortable initially consulting with their primary physician, who can offer a referral to an appropriate specialist. Due to the complexities Asperger's adds to any of these conditions, I recommend consulting with a specialist familiar with AS.

Helping Your Partner to Cope

You may want to help your partner with all of her struggles, and she might expect you to. The ways you can help your partner vary, depending on the strengths and weaknesses of both of you. I can offer some general guidelines.

* *Learn all you can about symptoms and treatment.* You can find information in books and online for all conditions listed here and their relationship to Asperger's syndrome.

* *Encourage and support treatment.* Early treatment improves prognosis. People with AS may lack insight into their condition or may recognize that something is wrong but not know where or how to reach out for help.

* *Be understanding.* Your partner cannot just "get over" his AS, or just snap out of a panic attack or depressive episode. Criticism tends to increase problems, but your understanding can help.

* *Be patient.* Getting better takes time, even with the best treatment; expect ups and downs. Managing symptoms can be a lifelong process for people with AS.

* *Reduce stress.* Stress affects both body and mind, and makes most symptoms worse. Encourage your partner to manage stress by eating well, getting enough sleep, exercising, and practicing relaxation techniques.

Coping with Your Partner's Co-existing Conditions

* *Reach out for support and help.* Confide in friends, relatives, or professionals.

* *Support your partner, but keep your own goals and priorities.* Maintain your personal plans, friendships, and activities as much as possible.

* *Be proactive.* Help your partner to know what triggers certain symptoms. You can help minimize them for her and your relationship.

* *Set boundaries.* This concerns what you can do without feeling overwhelmed and resentful. Letting Asperger's syndrome or any other condition take over your life is not healthy for you or your partner.

* *Accept your own limitations.* You cannot cure or rescue your partner from AS or any of the conditions that may go along with it.

* *Communicate honestly.* It's natural for you to feel angry and frustrated when your partner upsets you. Try not to express your emotions in ways you will regret, but do not hide them either. Talk honestly and lovingly before pent-up emotions interfere with your relationship.

* *Maintain calm.* If you become too emotional about your partner's difficulties, you both may feel out of control.

* *Use humor.* It can go a long way in helping you deal with difficult situations. Laugh with your partner but not at him; if he fails to see the humor in a situation, don't push it.

Every person with AS is unique, as is every relationship. These general guidelines should assist you in helping your partner to manage her symptoms and in maintaining your own mental health in the process. Specific symptoms also call for more specific strategies. Your partner's treatment may involve many more strategies than those offered here. The best treatment options will be tailored specifically for your partner. Being a supportive partner includes learning strategies to help your partner and to support ongoing treatment efforts.

Anxiety

Anxiety appears commonly among people with Asperger's syndrome. Many people with AS seem hardwired to worry from the outset. The stress of coping with confusing social expectations and demands of living can further increase anxiety.

Without treatment, anxiety can increasingly interfere with your relationship. Most commonly in people with AS, severe anxiety takes the form of generalized anxiety disorder, obsessive-compulsive disorder, social anxiety, or some combination.

Generalized Anxiety Disorder

Life brings myriad worries, doubts, and fears. The difference between "normal" worrying and *generalized anxiety disorder* (GAD) is that GAD causes exaggerated worry with no apparent rational cause. Symptoms can include muscle tension, stomach problems, irritability, difficulty concentrating, restlessness, and general fears. Your partner may have difficulty turning off anxious thoughts and relaxing. A mental health professional can help your partner learn to deal with worries more productively.

GENERALIZED ANXIETY IN YOUR PARTNER

"Aspergian" behavior, such as withdrawal, unusual body movements, and irritability, may increase during times of stress for your partner living with AS, who might:

* Worry too much and complain of feeling on edge

* Have a hard time sitting still or relaxing

* Talk excessively or very little

* Show increased fidgeting, pacing, or rigidity

* Withdraw more than usual, possibly retreating into his special interest

* Complain of sweating, having a pounding heart, or being confused

WHAT IT MEANS FOR YOUR RELATIONSHIP

Generalized anxiety disorder can be difficult to deal with, because the cause of anxiety or what to do to relieve your partner may not be clear. She may express constant worry and pace unrelentingly. There may be no apparent trigger for these feelings, making it easy to take your partner's preoccupation, withdrawal, or irritability personally.

Helping Your Partner to Cope with Generalized Anxiety

* *Help your partner to calm himself.* His sensory preferences and interests can help in suggesting what may calm him versus what may add to his stress or anxiety.

* *Remove pressure.* Too much pressure can increase anxiety. Offer to do some of the tasks that seem overwhelming for your partner.

* *Encourage certain activities.* Focus on activities that occupy your partner with something besides anxiety, such as playing an instrument, gardening, practicing yoga, or other activities that your partner enjoys.

* *Learn and practice relaxation and meditation techniques.* Do this with your partner if possible. Consider deep breathing and other meditative techniques that help to cope with anxiety symptoms.

Coping with Your Partner's Generalized Anxiety

* *Take a break.* Do this whenever you need to, by reading a book, taking a walk, calling a friend, and so on.

* *Encourage your partner to use other resources.* Your partner's therapist or a self-help book might help. You do not have to be there for your partner at your own expense.

* *Avoid certain situations.* When possible, avoid the situations that increase your partner's anxiety.

* *Be direct, strong, and positive.* Anxiety can interfere with your partner's ability to think rationally and calmly. Use your own rational thoughts and supportive actions to take control, make decisions, and stay calm.

Social Anxiety (Social Phobia)

An adult with *social anxiety*, or *social phobia*, shows an excessive fear of social situations. Nervousness and self-consciousness may develop from concern about others' potential judgment or criticism. Social anxiety increases for people with AS in situations where uncertainty exists about what to say or do, or when they do not want to receive negative feedback. People with AS can develop social anxiety from frequent putdowns and criticism. The more your partner practices anxiety-reducing techniques, such as relaxation and meditation, the more they help when needed in difficult situations.

SOCIAL ANXIETY IN YOUR PARTNER

If your partner with Asperger's experiences social anxiety, she may:

* Worry intensely before an upcoming social event

* Avoid social situations

* Experience self-consciousness and anxiety in social situations

* Spend increasing amounts of time alone

* Experience anxiety when just thinking about socializing

* Worry about how others perceive her, fearing judgment and criticism

WHAT IT MEANS FOR YOUR RELATIONSHIP

Relationships often spiral in an unwanted direction, because your partner increasingly may want to avoid going out with friends or to family events. He might express feeling awkward around others or might behave uncomfortably. He may leave the room during a social gathering, refrain from conversation, or choose to stay home altogether. Sometimes couples change plans at the last minute due to the AS partner's anxiety attack.

Helping Your Partner to Cope with Social Anxiety

* *Offer social guidance.* Your partner may seem charming in social situations, because the help she needs may be subtle. Many books and videos offer such help.

* *Encourage gradual social exposure.* Slowly meeting new people often helps people who have both AS and social anxiety to become more comfortable with others.

* *Help your partner aim for small social goals.* Support her when she feels discouraged.

* *Recognize your partner's real difficulty in trying new things.* Be supportive to help increase your partner's competence and confidence in social situations.

* *Offer positive feedback.* Lectures, criticism, and demands do not help someone change, and often make the person feel more anxious.

Coping with Your Partner's Social Anxiety

* *Be patient, but push for change.* Balance your partner's need to lean on you with his need for personal growth. Encourage gradual increases in his social responsibility.

* *Keep inviting your partner to come with you to social events.* Leaving him home so that you can enjoy yourself is also okay sometimes.

* *Compromise.* Avoid fighting with your partner to handle situations that remain too difficult right now.

* *Maintain your plans.* If your partner cannot join you, consider going alone or with a friend.

* *Manage your own emotions.* Staying in control when your partner becomes anxious helps you to feel calmer and helps your partner to be less fearful.

Obsessive-Compulsive Disorder

Obsessive-compulsive disorder (OCD) involves having upsetting and intrusive thoughts that are accompanied by compulsions, which are repetitive behaviors that someone feels driven to perform. Certain behaviors in Asperger's syndrome mimic OCD, such as lining up shoes, eating the same meal every day, and the tendency to become obsessed with certain ideas, objects, and activities. With OCD the person is more likely to recognize her thoughts as obsessive and acknowledge the compulsive nature of the acts that must be performed, such as excessive hand washing, checking, counting, or arranging things in order.

In OCD the thoughts and behaviors don't bring pleasure the way typical activities and preoccupations often do for the person with AS. In Asperger's syndrome, the preoccupations often help the person cope with anxiety, while preoccupations in OCD stem from and often create more anxiety.

OBSESSIVE-COMPULSIVE DISORDER IN YOUR PARTNER

If your partner struggles with OCD, he may:

* Complain of upsetting and intruding thoughts

* Show excessive concern about germs and contamination

* Fear hurting himself or others without showing evidence of aggression

* Count, tap, or perform other seemingly senseless behaviors

* Arrange certain items methodically, or check and recheck them

* Hoard unnecessary items

WHAT IT MEANS FOR YOUR RELATIONSHIP

Your partner's world may shrink as she focuses on obsessions and compulsive behaviors. Feeling controlled by strange behaviors may make your partner with AS behave irritably and insist on having things her way to an increasingly intolerable point. Your partner's preoccupations may interfere significantly with your ability to compromise and communicate as a couple. The following strategies can help, whether your partner demonstrates OCD-like behaviors or a full-blown case of OCD.

Helping Your Partner to Cope with Obsessive-Compulsive Disorder

* *Practice skills learned in therapy designed to help eliminate obsessions and compulsions.* They will be difficult for your partner, so do them together, when possible, to help him follow through.

* *Maintain routines that make it harder for the OCD to take over.* Obsessions and compulsions can consume life. Your partner may already tend toward isolation due to AS.

* *Encourage your partner to practice relaxation and stress relief techniques for anxiety.* Some possibilities might include yoga, mindfulness meditation, and deep breathing, which can also reduce symptoms of anxiety brought on by OCD.

* *Refrain from participating in rituals or offering constant reassurance.* Both of these actions make obsessions worse by giving them credibility.

Coping with Your Partner's Obsessive-Compulsive Disorder

* *Do not let OCD take over your life.* Don't make it too easy for your partner to give in to OCD demands.

* *Help your partner.* Encourage her to gradually overcome obsessions and rituals one at a time, beginning with the easiest first and working slowly.

* *Acknowledge when your partner resists OCD behaviors.* Support and encourage this.

Refusing to participate in OCD behavior proves much easier said than done, especially if the behaviors become part of your relationship. But you can manage OCD and, along with it, your relationship. Do not hesitate to seek help from someone with experience in this area.

Depression

Common symptoms of depression include overwhelming sadness, withdrawal, helplessness, hopelessness, difficulty concentrating, and possible thoughts of death or suicide. Along with other factors that contribute to depression, difficulty fitting in and not understanding the social world can lead to depression in people with Asperger's syndrome. As Tony Attwood (2007a) points out, the self-respect of many people with autism becomes negatively affected by lifelong experiences of misunderstanding, ridicule, and rejection.

DEPRESSION IN YOUR PARTNER

If your partner with Asperger's syndrome experiences depression, he may:

* Experience low moods, possibly with tearfulness

* Report low energy or feeling fatigued

* Have little interest in activities he usually enjoys

* Express low-self esteem

* Show changes in sleep, appetite, behavior, or a combination of these areas

* Take less care of personal hygiene than usual

WHAT IT MEANS FOR YOUR RELATIONSHIP

When depressed, your partner may seem disinterested in you or in usual activities, and this can cause you feelings of rejection or abandonment. In addition to your partner's usual AS behaviors that can leave you feeling abandoned, a depressed partner feels depleted and can deplete you as well.

Helping Your Partner to Cope with Depression

* *Don't take it personally.* Your partner may push you away, even losing interest in sex.

* *Offer to help out with household responsibilities.* Everyday tasks may be overwhelming for your partner to manage.

* *Encourage activity.* Suggest walks or other exercise. Be persistent but not unreasonable in trying to get your partner up and out.

* *Let your partner talk.* Discuss whatever she wants, including suicide. Depression distorts thought and judgment, so rather than increasing the risk, talking can help protect her. You can find valuable resources on the Internet to help you both

cope. If your partner expresses suicidal intent, seek immediate professional help.

Coping with Your Partner's Depression

* *Be supportive, within reason.* Don't try to handle it alone. Reach out to others.

* *Continue the activities you enjoy.* Depression can be contagious; try not to get dragged down with your partner.

* *Enforce your personal boundaries.* Try to get your partner up and out, but get up and out with or without him.

* *Remember that you did not cause your partner's depression.* You cannot be responsible for curing him of it.

Attention Deficit Disorder

Attention deficit disorder (ADD), with or without hyperactivity (ADHD), often presents additional struggles for people with Asperger's. This condition is often present as a part of AS. The symptoms of ADHD fall into two broad categories: inattention and hyperactivity. Inattention can include poor attention to details, difficulty focusing on tasks, and procrastination. Hyperactivity or impulsive behavior includes restlessness and poor self-control. Symptoms of ADD or ADHD may affect your partner's motivation and executive functioning, which includes her ability to organize thoughts and activities, prioritize, manage time, and make decisions.

ATTENTION DIFFICULTIES IN YOUR PARTNER

If your partner with Asperger's syndrome also experiences attention problems, he may:

* Appear fidgety, pace, or interrupt others

* Tend to be forgetful and easily distractible, losing items

* Have difficulty focusing or paying close attention

* Experience poor self-control

* Procrastinate or show impulsive behavior

* Struggle with household tasks or organization

WHAT IT MEANS FOR YOUR RELATIONSHIP

Your partner's inattention can include careless mistakes, difficulty following instructions, and procrastination, all of which can cause you to feel tuned out or uncared for. Hyperactivity can include a range of problems, from annoying interruptions to impulsive spending that negatively affects your budget and finances.

Helping Your Partner with Attention Difficulties

* *Use written communication techniques.* Doing so will help your partner keep track of what needs to be done and when.

* *Encourage your partner to exercise daily.* This helps to work off excess energy and improve mood. Sleep and diet are essential for optimal brain and body functioning.

* *Break down large tasks into smaller, more manageable ones.* This can help your partner avoid getting overwhelmed.

* *Encourage your partner to regularly practice relaxation techniques.* Doing so can greatly reduce symptoms of ADD or ADHD, and may help your partner to control both attention and impulses.

Coping with Your Partner's Attention Difficulties

* *Divide tasks realistically.* Doing chores together may help your partner stay on task and keep you from getting frustrated when tasks remain incomplete.

* *Choose your battles.* Nagging, threatening, or yelling rarely improves an undesirable situation.

* *Maintain boundaries.* Do not allow your partner's inattention or impulsivity to interfere with your own goals and plans; protect your personal well-being.

Bipolar Disorder

Many people with Asperger's syndrome show mood changes and difficulty controlling moods. *Bipolar disorder* involves high (manic) and low (depressed) moods that cycle over periods of time. Changes in energy level, sleep, and thought patterns can also occur and can involve distress and disruption. In a manic phase, your partner may have a surprisingly high self-esteem or sense of power (grandiosity). Her mood may be noticeably improved, or her behavior may become more aggressive than usual; meltdowns may increase, or she can seem overly upbeat and excitable.

BIPOLAR DISORDER IN YOUR PARTNER

If your partner with Asperger's syndrome struggles with bipolar disorder, he may:

* Have moods that seem to cycle from high to low and low to high

* Sometimes show the signs listed under depression

* At other times, show increased energy levels and less need for sleep

* Show unpredictable changes in mood or self-esteem

* Have racing thoughts and distractibility

* Show excessive involvement in pleasurable activities

WHAT IT MEANS FOR YOUR RELATIONSHIP

People who have both Asperger's syndrome and bipolar disorder can cycle between periods of success and creativity, and periods of immobilizing depression. Your partner may cycle from feeling worthless and suicidal, to feeling invincible and making poor decisions that have serious consequences for your relationship. If your partner's moods seem to cycle dramatically up and down, it could be worth seeking help from a psychologist or psychiatrist for possible bipolar disorder.

Helping Your Partner to Cope with Bipolar Disorder

* *Expect mood changes.* Agree on a specific action plan for difficult times, such as going together to the doctor, or holding on to the checks and credit cards.

* *Make a list of emergency contact information.* Include doctors, therapists, and others who can help during a crisis.

* *Try to spend positive time with your partner.* Walk off her excess energy together.

* *Avoid extra stimulation.* Keep your surroundings as quiet as possible.

Coping with Your Partner's Bipolar Disorder

* *Avoid heated discussions or disagreement during mood swings.* During a manic phase, your partner may show aggression or embarrass you; when depressed, he may appear pessimistic and irritable.

* *Go out for a while.* Plan where to go when you need to separate yourself temporarily.

* *Maintain boundaries.* This will protect your own mental health.

* *Try to avoid situations that might increase your partner's irritability.* Such situations could make it more difficult for him to cope.

Sensory Processing and Integration

Variations in neurology cause all kinds of variations in learning, understanding, thinking, feeling, and behaving. Sensory problems and various learning disabilities frequently appear with Asperger's syndrome. *Sensory processing* refers to the way the brain receives and understands information from our senses. Difficulties integrating or processing sensory information appear to be widespread among people with Asperger's syndrome, leading to problems with receiving, organizing, or making use of sensory information.

Everyone experiences differences in sensory processing; all of us have certain likes and dislikes when it comes to smells, sounds, sight, touch, and taste. Due to sensory processing or integration issues, your partner with AS may have extreme sensitivity to certain experiences. She may constantly deal with overwhelming amounts of sensory input or may interpret sensations differently than you do. Background voices in a restaurant, for example, may make it difficult to focus on a single conversation.

Certain fabrics, foods, or sounds may constitute what Stephen Shore (2002) refers to as "sensory violations," and can be absolutely intolerable for your partner. On the other end, some people with AS have undersensitivity to sensory information and a high threshold for pain. These people may seek extra stimulation through activities like rocking, spinning, or applying deep pressure to parts of their bodies. Sensory overload can overwhelm your partner and affect the quality of your interactions together. Avoiding offensive sensory situations may lead your partner to rigidly stick to certain experiences, such as what foods to eat or where to dine out.

SENSORY ISSUES IN YOUR PARTNER

If a sensory condition affects your partner with Asperger's syndrome, he may:

* Be overly sensitive to certain sights, sounds, textures, smells, or tastes

* Enjoy deep pressure, spinning, or rocking

* Show poor coordination or lack of balance

* Have difficulty with handwriting

* Avoid or overreact to touch

WHAT IT MEANS FOR YOUR RELATIONSHIP

Many people with AS learn to compensate when they encounter sensory experiences they find offensive. If necessary, you and your partner can brainstorm about helpful ways to deal with your partner's specific sensory variations and difficulties.

Helping Your Partner to Cope with Sensory Issues

* *Your partner can learn personal triggers and ways to adjust or compensate.* Small accommodations based on your partner's specific sensitivities can make a big difference.

* *When sensitivity affects hygiene, you can find creative solutions.* For example, consider buying soaps with varying smells and textures to find one that your partner will use consistently, or buy more than one of his favorite shirts so it can be washed more often.

* *Encourage quiet time.* This might especially apply when your partner seems overwhelmed by the sensory experiences and violations of everyday life.

Coping with Your Partner's Sensory Issues

* *Try to avoid what violates your partner's senses, once you know what that is.* If you cannot avoid potential sensory violations, give your partner a heads-up concerning what to expect.

* *Look for patterns.* Your partner may not be able to explain what bothers her; pay attention to times and places that seem to increase agitation.

* *Don't take hypersensitivity personally.* If your partner experiences a certain touch as offensive, it has nothing to do with her feelings of affection toward you.

Substance Use and Abuse

Alcohol, tranquilizers, and stimulant drugs, among other substances, can provide relief for uncomfortable social situations and awkward feelings. The tendency of people with AS to spend time alone and to repeat pleasurable behaviors may add to the addictive quality that certain drugs may hold. Signs of drug or alcohol abuse include neglecting responsibilities due to substance use, driving under the influence, having legal trouble that results from substance use, and experiencing relationship problems, such as fights, due to behavioral changes while under the influence. Addiction must be treated before you can work effectively on your relationship.

Helping Your Partner with a Substance Abuse Problem

* *Avoid threatening, lecturing, or crying.* These reactions usually increase guilt and the excuse to drink or use drugs.

* *Let your partner know your concerns.* Offer help and support in dealing with the abuse and finding appropriate treatment. Use specific examples of his behavior to deal with excuses and denial.

* *Don't cover up or make excuses for your partner's behavior.* Don't try to protect him from the consequences.

* *Be clear that your partner will need treatment.* This should include new coping skills to help in overcoming a serious drinking or drug problem.

Coping with Your Partner's Substance Abuse Problem

* *Focus on your own needs.* Don't allow your partner's problem with substance abuse to become the focus of your own life and happiness.

* *You can support your partner.* You can encourage treatment, but you can't force change; your partner's acceptance of responsibility and seeking help constitute essential steps in her addiction recovery.

* *Don't take over your partner's responsibilities.* That would leave her with no sense of importance and makes continued use too easy.

* *Avoid arguing when your partner seems under the influence.* Separate yourself if necessary.

* *Join a support group.* Support groups for family members coping with addiction can be very helpful. Reach out to friends, family, professionals, or your faith community.

Points to Keep in Mind

According to the National Institute of Mental Health, depression, anxiety, and substance abuse often occur together (Regier et al. 1998). These and other conditions associated with Asperger's need attention and treatment so that they don't develop further and complicate the syndrome. They must sometimes be treated first, so that your partner can be productive and successful in work and love. In other cases, the co-occurring conditions can be treated along with the distressing symptoms of AS.

The prognosis for co-occurring conditions depends on many factors, including the severity of the condition and the strength of personal resources; a supportive partner can make a big difference. Above all, take all symptoms of your partner's struggles seriously. Kelly has had AS and depression for as long as she can remember. She used to sit at home in the dark for hours. Usually, her mom would come in at some point to open window shades and turn on lights, exclaiming, "Don't sit in the dark! Depressed people sit in the dark!" Kelly didn't receive treatment for depression until many years later, and she feels resentment about this. Turning on the lights never made Kelly feel less depressed. In fact, she felt misunderstood, which added to her depression.

Acknowledging your partner's struggles and providing support prove most helpful in navigating a life together with Asperger's syndrome and its potential co-occurring conditions. Ask your partner what he needs from you to help him through difficult times, rather than assuming that you know. Focus on the reasons you fell in love: your partner's unique talents, accomplishments, and positive attributes.

CHAPTER 12

Irreconcilable Differences

Some of us think holding on makes us strong;
but sometimes it is letting go.

—Hermann Hesse

Sometimes partners end up going their separate ways. In my work with couples, I focus on keeping partnerships together whenever possible. But by the time some couples come for help, they already find it too difficult to get beyond the built-up sadness and contempt. The anger and resentment can become so intense that the partners can no longer work positively together.

You chose your partner, but you may not have chosen the depth of the challenges in your relationship to someone with Asperger's syndrome. Your relationship expectations and your relationship reality may be irreconcilable.

I recommend that you do everything you can to change yourself and your relationship in a positive direction. You may regret ending a relationship if you don't truly believe you did everything you could to fix the problems. If your partner remains unable or unwilling to set goals, to communicate productively, or to otherwise work with you toward a mutually satisfying relationship, she may be sending a message that you need to hear. When a couple cannot work together after trying as much as they can, I help the partners to separate as amicably as possible.

Consider Yourself

You may have avoided problems or red flags early on in order to give your relationship time to grow and improve. Some of the very things that attracted you in the beginning may be the undoing of your relationship. Your partner just loved hanging out with you; now he bores you and never wants to go anywhere. He seemed brilliant and knew so much; now he just keeps talking about the same topic until you can no longer listen.

As I mentioned in chapter 6, as long as productive work remains, you can keep working—with or without your partner. When you run out of genuinely helpful work that you can do alone and your partner shows an inability or unwillingness to participate, your relationship stagnates. It may be time for you to take an honest look and make a decision: do you want to remain in the relationship, or take action to adequately get your needs met and live a more fulfilling life?

In working through this book, you have set goals, both large and small, and decided on small steps for achieving them. There may be a limit to how long you can wait to get what you need. Only you can decide whether you can continue to tolerate your situation, and whether you still have the energy to try to make it work. Can you stay and keep working to rekindle and deepen the love between you and your partner?

Considering a Breakup

Relationship partners may consider ending their partnership at various points in their relationship. Sometimes people stay in a relationship longer than they should because they feel a certain comfort despite their unhappiness. Your partner with Asperger's syndrome may offer few demands and leave you alone to do your own thing. Of course, this can also be why you considered leaving in the first place. You might also feel guilty for wanting to end a relationship for reasons having to do with AS.

AMBIVALENCE

Ambivalence results when you feel contradictory feelings about something. The love you have shared and the memories of good times together, coupled with day-to-day annoyances and loneliness, cause ambivalence for many partners. No matter how much you hate your partner, you probably also still love her in many ways. Even if you no longer love her, you don't want to hurt your partner, because you do care about her. Ambivalence about your partner makes it hard to make a decision about whether to stay or leave.

Sometimes people in such a situation make a pro-and-con list to try to figure out what to do. You can do this if you find it helpful—though it doesn't always help when you feel ambivalent, since ambivalent feelings tend to fluctuate back and forth. Your pro-and-con list may change as your feelings do, depending on your mood or current feeling about your partner. Fear of change or concern for a partner also keeps people in relationships that they might otherwise end.

Other common reasons partners give for not feeling free to end their relationships include:

* *My partner with AS needs me.* You have to decide whether you want to be in an unbalanced relationship. Make sure your partner has support if you believe he needs it.

* *My partner loves me and has no idea I want to end it; this will surprise and "kill" him.* Perhaps your partner has no clue that you want out or about the relationship issues that make you want to leave. Maybe you have tried to tell him and have tried to work on such issues, but for some reason, he doesn't understand or get it. If you no longer have strong feelings about your partner, guilt is not a good reason to stay.

* *What will my family and friends think?* Many people worry about this before things get so bad that it no longer matters what other people think. Do what you must to get what you genuinely need; you are worthy of a fulfilling relationship.

* *How can I leave my partner? He has a disorder, and I should be here to help him through it.* Asperger's syndrome affects all kinds of people with all kinds of personalities. If you decide to leave, do so because your partner will not or cannot try to meet your needs, not because he has AS. It doesn't make sense to stay just because your partner has Asperger's, and it doesn't make sense to leave just because of it either.

* *Why can I not accept my partner for himself, as he accepts me?* Considering leaving because you can't get your needs met in your relationship does not mean that you do not accept your partner for being himself. You understand AS and still chose to remain with your partner to this point. The main issue now concerns the fact that you have needs too.

* *What about the kids?* Both divorces and unhappy relationships can be potentially harmful for children. Studies show that parental conflict or destructive behavior affects children negatively whether the parents stay together or not (Wallerstein and Blakeslee 2003). You hold responsibility for making sure that your relationship does not damage your children, whether you stay or go.

Even in abusive situations, such as when your partner repeatedly and deliberately hurts you in either emotional or physical ways, the need to end a relationship often gets emotionally clouded.

Your partner once made you feel excited on your most boring days. But do you constantly feel down about where things are now? Working with a professional may also help you sort through your confusion, analyze your situation, and make a rational decision. By trying everything you can think of and then trying some more, you will be clear about your decision and less likely to second-guess yourself later. Take a few minutes to write in your journal about what it would be like to end your relationship. What would your life be like? Write your future story.

POSSIBLE SIGNS THAT IT'S OVER

Do you feel resentful and exhausted when you think about dealing with your partner's point of view or your need to relate to her in a more structured, rational way? Your relationship may be more than you bargained for, and more than you can or want to continue working at. It may seriously be time to end your relationship if you find yourself:

* *Doing all of the relationship work.* You and your partner may both say that you want to improve your relationship, but then you both have to work at it. Due to your partner's Asperger's syndrome, you probably do more of the relationship work. But you can't do it all on your own. If, after you have tried everything, your partner still does not participate with you in any way, you may want to consider moving on.

* *Feeling empty or lonely most of the time.* If you can't foresee this changing, you may consider the need to leave.

* *Experiencing abuse of any kind.* Any abuse, be it physical or emotional, can be a major red flag for the future of your relationship; at the very least, abuse should not be tolerated.

* *Losing your sense of self.* This may have occurred over the course of this relationship if you have changed your core values, beliefs, and goals to accommodate your partner. If you changed completely in order to live with your partner in his reality, it may be time to take your life back.

* *Feeling deep frustration about your relationship.* This would especially apply if too many of your basic and most important emotional needs are not being met.

DECIDING TO PART

Ending a relationship almost always proves difficult, but sometimes it is the right thing to do. As with other experiences in life, it doesn't work to avoid or deny the situation between you and your partner. Ending relationships tends to be associated with failure, but there is no need for blame or judgment. Carrying rage, criticism, or dishonesty hurts all involved and can damage your self-esteem.

Even if you choose to end your relationship, it is still a loss and it still hurts. Death is one of the hardest facts of life, and the end of a relationship is one of the hardest facts of love. As painful as a relationship ending can be, the process can be a source of learning and personal growth.

Ending Your Relationship

Once you decide to end your relationship, there may be some unique concerns to consider in breaking up with someone with Asperger's syndrome. By now, you probably know your partner well enough to know how she might react. Choose a time and place that will allow both of you room to discuss the situation and relate to each other about it.

Some of the same AS traits that made the relationship difficult can make the ending difficult too. For example, some partners with Asperger's don't know how to talk about the sadness or anger that they may feel when they find out you want to leave them. They may not know what questions to ask or how to fight for the relationship.

Many relationships end with the non-AS partner feeling as if she were the abandoned or rejected one, even though she initiated the breakup. Your AS partner may listen to what you say and sadly accept the relationship's ending. On the other hand, he may feel hurt and angry. He may get upset and yell, or say mean things to you. Try not to argue or get too defensive. Continue to show love and compassion, regardless of how he reacts. Your partner's reaction may be one of the hardest steps in the ending process, but it's important for both of you in making closure and starting again.

An Approach to Splitting Up

A rational and thoughtful approach may be a helpful way to discuss your relationship's ending. Write down the reasons why you believe your relationship must end. Communicate your reasons clearly and respectfully. Approach your partner honestly, and be ready with behavioral observations and rational answers to questions.

The irony, in the case of a partner with AS, is that it may actually hurt more when you present logical or rational reasons; your partner will understand your rationale on a different level than a tearful, hysterical breakup. But it will hurt more only because she understands it better, and her understanding will be helpful to both of you in moving on. Focus on the needs you have that continue unmet in your current relationship. Be as clear and rational as you can. Give your partner time to absorb the information you offer. Listen while she expresses her own concerns and frustrations with you about the relationship or your decision to end it.

RESPECT STILL MATTERS

No matter what point the relationship has come to, your partner continues to be someone you have loved, and probably still do love. When love is not enough and the relationship ends, you can still treat each other with respect. Honesty shows respect and love, and really is the best policy. Let your partner know about things you learned from the relationship and things about him that you appreciate. If you are truly ready for your relationship to end, though, don't confuse your partner with your ambivalence.

Starting Over

Your behavior in one relationship, including how you end it, affects your behavior in the next one. If the suggestions in this book did not help you to improve your current relationship, I hope they succeeded in helping you to improve your future relationships. Following the tips and suggestions presented, and understanding both your conscious and unconscious reasons for ending up in this relationship, you can step forward into future relationships with more awareness.

EXERCISE 12.1   My Ideal Relationship

This exercise helps you think about what you need in a partner and in a relationship. It prepares you to make a new beginning and go for your ideal relationship.

1.   Take the time to think about what traits you would like in a partner on a day-to-day basis. This should not be a reaction to your current partner, but your dream for the future.

2. In your journal or on a separate piece of paper, write down all the characteristics of your ideal partner and what you want to get from your next relationship.

3. Keep this list and refer to it. Don't lose sight of what you need and hope for.

4. Be prepared for your next relationship to be imperfect. It may meet more of your needs than the current one, but all partnerships require work and compromise.

Hopefully, you learned a lot from your relationship and from the work you did to try to improve it. Once you decide to leave, take some time to regroup. Jumping into a new relationship too soon might risk your repeating some of the same patterns that began or ended this partnership. Write in your journal about what you learned in this relationship that you want to take with you and apply to the next one. Keep your personal goals in mind as you follow your heart and look to fulfill your dreams.

Points to Keep in Mind

If you cannot find a way to bridge the gap of the differences between you and your partner, or if you just don't have the energy or love that it would take anymore, it may be time to move on. If you don't experience your current relationship as meeting your important relationship needs, take an honest look at making a serious change. For this, you must examine your ambivalence and the varying beliefs that work to keep you in a place where you no longer want to be.

If you recognize major problems in your relationship but continue having difficulty making the decision about whether to stay together or break up, it might be helpful to seek the advice of knowledgeable friends, family members, or a professional. Doing so can sometimes be part of trying every option so that you don't harbor guilt and second-guess your-self once you finally make a decision and take the next step in your life. You have a right to get your important needs met and live a satisfying life in a mutually satisfying relationship.

CHAPTER 13

Choosing to Stay

There is no remedy for love but to love more.

—Henry David Thoreau

Relationships that include someone with Asperger's syndrome can be happy and satisfying. You and your partner fell in love for a reason. You can continue moving toward the intimate relationship and the life together that you really want.

Most of this book is about choosing to stay in your relationship and the work that it might take to make it more deeply fulfilling for you and your partner. In this chapter, I review some of the important points you need to keep in mind as you go forward. In doing this, I also help you to create an explicit contract for you and your partner to follow from here on. Based on a new definition of "happily ever after," you and your partner will negotiate your relationship contract and go forward in love together.

If You Had Only Known

Many partners go about their lives with an unwritten partnership contract and neglect to openly discuss expectations and responsibilities. This agreement that you made with your partner in the beginning probably needs renegotiating at this point in your relationship. There is more than one way to live in a strong and happy partnership. Various models of relationship can work, just as various models of parenting and friendship work. If it works for the two of you, it's a fine partnership.

The partnership that works for you and your partner may not work for any other partnership. Being in a relationship that meets the needs of both partners and that changes as each of you and your relationship change matters the most. Other people's opinions about the ways that you and your partner relate to each other may be based on irrelevant assumptions, and may not apply to the two of you.

Your Relationship Contract

To make valuable progress in your partnership together, you have to communicate and respect each other's differences. Both you and your partner bring positive characteristics and qualities to your relationship. It's important for you both to listen and be open to each other. Each of you must be willing to work toward getting your own and the other's needs met. Your new relationship contract should focus on the needs of both of you and making your relationship mutually satisfying.

Most people don't have an actual written agreement, although it does help some people with Asperger's and their partners. You and your partner have to decide what works for you. If you're not sure, give it a try. You can also discuss needs and goals without writing things down, if you prefer, as long as you cover all of the important topics and make your needs and expectations explicit. A typed, informal summary can help you both remember the important points of what you talked about. A written summary can also serve as a starting point when you sit down to discuss how your goals and dreams hold up six months or a year later.

EXERCISE 13.1   Relationship Agreement

You can develop a personalized relationship agreement based on the model shown here. Doing so sometimes helps partners to remember the importance of meeting relationship needs and goals, and provides concrete evidence of continued commitment. In working on our relationship together, we promise to:

1. Listen with sincerity. We agree to try hard to understand each other's perspective.

2. Communicate honestly, giving clear directions concerning what we want and how to provide it.

Current Goals

Sal	Andy
I will work hard to eliminate the following three behaviors that bother you:	
Eating alone	Nagging about your spending time alone
Not greeting you when I come home	Following you when you want to be alone
Never going out to dinner	Refusing to cook if you won't go out to eat
I will continue to do the following three things that you really like:	
Fold your clothes for you	Bring home chocolates
Send a text message at least once a day	Send you research articles via e-mail
Make music CDs for you	Keep your car filled with fuel

Finances

All financial decisions involving over 100 dollars will be discussed and agreed on. We will not accrue any more bills without discussing it first.

Our signatures represent our sincere intentions to follow this relationship agreement. Problems in following this agreement will be raised as they occur in order to give each other a chance to change.

This contract will be reviewed and renegotiated within six months from the date of our signatures.

Sal Blank   Andy Who

_____ Date: _____   _____ Date: _____

You can have as many categories as make sense for you and your partner. You can sit together once or twice a year to review your partnership vision, whether goals are continuing to be met, whether you want to add new goals, and so forth. You can also attach supplemental sheets to your contract that include additional personal or partnership goals and your plans for achieving them, though I do not recommend working on too many goals at once. You and your partner will meet with more success when you have a clear agreement that seems truly doable for both of you.

Relationship Happiness

It may be helpful to remember that no one person can fulfill all of your needs. Life is full of ups and downs, and life after you have joined a partnership continues to present new, wonderful, and challenging experiences. Living happily ever after with a partner does not mean being happy all the time. It does mean sharing your life, with all of its unexpected twists and turns, with someone you love, who loves you. What else does it mean to you?

EXERCISE 13.2 Redefining "Happily Ever After"

In this structured exercise, you and your partner will consider your goals and dreams based on your current understanding of Asperger's syndrome, each other, and your relationship.

1. Write at least a paragraph about what happiness with your partner means to you. If you don't like writing, give this some serious thought, and take notes if you have to, in order to have a meaningful discussion with your partner.

2. Discuss and share with your partner your goals and dreams for your life together. They can be as simple as the wish to own a house together and put aside enough money to enjoy retirement, or they can be more complicated, with shared visions about future travel or life changes.

3. Listen to your partner with your heart as you continue to use your own ingenuity to reach for the changes that will bring you a deeper sense of security and love.

Points to Keep in Mind

Change can start anywhere. You can change your thinking and attitudes, behavior, or feelings, and no matter where you begin, it will affect both you and your partner in some way. One partner cannot change without influencing the other; it's like a chemical equation in human terms. You may have become tired of being the one it always falls on to understand, compromise, and ultimately be responsible in your relationship. Consider that when you bent over backward to relate to your partner, you lacked certain important information about your partner's viewpoint. Learning the language you need to help your partner understand you and what you tried to say all along may be the key that makes the difference now.

A shared vision for your life partnership can hold you together, even through hard times. Working together on your common interests and goals can help you and your partner to continue to form a more solid basis for your partnership. Maintaining your personal goals remains critical for you, although working toward and reaching your relationship goals can also be highly energizing. When you meet shared goals, you get to share the excitement.

CHAPTER 14

Toward a New Partnership

Where thou art, that is home.

—Emily Dickinson

All of us change and grow. Your relationship is a work in progress now, and it may always be a work in progress. The little things you do for each other to show love and appreciation add up. Forming a healthier and more fulfilling partnership involves taking into account your overall strengths and weaknesses as individuals and as a couple.

The Human Spectrum

A wide range of "normal" behavior and "normal" relationships exists. Remember to think of the human spectrum and all of its diversity. You and your partner may each hold personal goals that are very different from the other person's. You may wish for an equal partner who shares equal responsibilities. Your partner with AS may want a partner who can take care of the many things that come so hard for her. Your partnership needs to be updated, changed, evaluated, and renegotiated now and throughout your relationship for the two of you to keep on top of changing needs.

Acknowledging Asperger's

Asperger's syndrome offers various strengths and weaknesses in your relationship. When you focus on the strengths and make your expectations realistic, your partner may feel less pressure, which might help him to relate more positively to you. Your understanding of AS will offer relief, whether your partner can change with you or not.

You and your partner need to acknowledge Asperger's syndrome and the differences between the two of you that result from it. According to Tony Attwood (1998), successful relationships in which one partner has AS show three similar characteristics:

* Both partners are aware of and acknowledge the Asperger's diagnosis.

* Both partners demonstrate motivation to make the relationship work; in particular, the AS partner shows willingness to accept certain guidance from her partner.

* The couple has access to a knowledgeable counselor who understands AS and its role in relationship issues.

Your partner may have difficulty with his role in your relationship. You can help by offering social and relationship understanding. It helps if you make the implicit rules that you live by in your partnership explicit, and renegotiate when necessary.

Change Begins with You

For many relationship systems, the chemistry equation works just this way: your increasing positive responses lead to your partner having increasing positive responses. It can be very difficult to respond positively to something your partner does that you do not like. But it can be worth forcing yourself through such a situation, because changing your response will quite possibly end up changing hers.

In addition, your partner with Asperger's syndrome may require one more step. If you stop responding negatively to your partner, the change in him may simply be to feel calmer and happier, because the tension has decreased. This may not result in any other desired change in his behavior. Your indirect cues to change may not be effective at all. However, with a calmer and more loving atmosphere, your partner may be better able to listen to your constructive criticism or feedback. If your partner feels appreciated and successful, he will more likely try to live up to your positive expectations of him, as long as he understands them. If he feels that he can never do anything right anyway or cannot meet your standards no matter how hard he tries, he may stop trying.

Be the Change

Make your life what you want it to be. If you want change, you must start by changing yourself. Move in ways that offer you more of what you need with your partner, along with your own growth and independence. It takes time and real staying power for you to learn about yourself and about your partner, to reinterpret your partner's behavior, and to learn to speak your partner's language. But this process contains the path to relating more fully and getting more of your needs met.

PROCEED WITH PATIENCE AND LOVE

In trying to change yourself, you can see how difficult and uncomfortable change can feel. Your partner with Asperger's syndrome may have an even harder time making changes than you do. Be patient and persistent with your own changes, and continue to offer your partner patience and understanding, as well as guidance about what to change and how to do it.

The more nonjudgmental you can be with your partner, the better she can pay attention to you and your feedback. Taking the pressure off of your partner can help her change and help both of you to feel less tension. You may be disappointed that certain seemingly simple things do not come naturally to her, but having to teach her beats settling for not getting what you want or her doing the wrong thing—again.

If you have followed the suggestions in this book, some changes have likely already begun happening in your relationship. They may be very small changes. Major changes will happen more slowly. Keep in mind that problems and obstacles are likely. When your relationship hits obstacles, be careful not to interpret you, your relationship, or your partner as failures. You may need to readjust, but problems don't constitute evidence that things will never change. Take obstacles as a signal in your relationship that you need to heed in order to readjust, renegotiate, and try again.

LEAVING RESENTMENT BEHIND

As you learn to understand your partner and how Asperger's complicates your relationship, you may need to work through valid feelings of sadness, anger, and resentment. This process is ongoing. Try not to let feelings about past experiences interfere with your commitment to the partnership of now and the future. These feelings will resurface from time to time, but staying angry at your partner for things that neither of you fully understood seems unfair. Your partner could not do what he could not understand or what didn't make sense to him. Learn from the past, but continue forward into your future. Focus now on a different relationship with your partner.

Reach Out

Your own health, happiness, and well-being are crucial to keep in mind as you work through the many issues in your relationship. It may help you to join an online forum or local support group for partners of people with AS, in which you can share experiences and reduce feelings of isolation and frustration. Some of these groups are listed in the "Helpful Resources" section in the back of the book. It's important for you to develop and maintain a lifestyle in which you take care of yourself and get your needs met in whatever reasonable way you can. Please consider seeking help from a mental health professional if you ever feel that you need it.

The State of the Union

Overall, additional research will help us learn what helps people with Asperger's and their intimate partners to live in healthy and happy partnerships with each other, as well as what hurts their ability to do this. The Interactive Autism Network collects information in a large database that may eventually offer needed information about relationships involving at least one partner with AS (www.iancommunity.org). Personal stories and anecdotes give us most of our current information about such relationships. Research could help us to understand relationship strengths and weaknesses, specific stressors and relationship difficulties, and the male and female differences that exist in relationships with AS. The more we learn, the more we can help partners like you to work on your relationship with the person you love who has Asperger's syndrome.

Choose Love

Your relationship has grown through certain personal choices you have made along the way. If you don't like the way things have developed in your current relationship, you can make other choices. You can choose to focus on getting your needs met and enjoying your intimate relationship and the life you have made with your current partner. You and your partner may have a long way to go, but you have now begun to move closer to the love you need and hope for. It's inside you. Remember how you felt about your partner once upon a time?

Helpful Resources

*What do we live for, if it is not to make life less
difficult for each other?*

—George Eliot

This section presents a compilation of resources for further help and information on Asperger's and relationships. The list includes books, websites, and organizations that address areas of probable interest to you in loving someone with Asperger's syndrome.

Books

TO HELP YOU LEARN MORE ABOUT ASPERGER'S

Ariel, C. N., and R. A. Naseef, eds. 2006. *Voices from the Spectrum: Parents, Grandparents, Siblings, People with Autism, and Professionals Share Their Wisdom.* London: Jessica Kingsley Publishers.

Attwood, T. 2007. *The Complete Guide to Asperger's Syndrome.* London: Jessica Kingsley Publishers.

Baron-Cohen, S. 2003. *The Essential Difference: Male and Female Brains and the Truth about Autism.* New York: Basic Books.

Gaus, V. L. 2011. *Living Well on the Spectrum: How to Use Your Strengths to Meet the Challenges of Asperger Syndrome / High-Functioning Autism.* New York: The Guilford Press.

Hénault, I. 2006. *Asperger's Syndrome and Sexuality: From Adolescence through Adulthood.* London: Jessica Kingsley Publishers.

Ortiz, J. M. 2008. *The Myriad Gifts of Asperger's Syndrome.* London: Jessica Kingsley Publishers.

Shore, S., and L. G. Rastelli. 2006. *Understanding Autism for Dummies.* Hoboken, NJ: Wiley Publishing.

Simone, R. 2010. *Aspergirls: Empowering Females with Asperger Syndrome.* London: Jessica Kingsley Publishers.

ABOUT INTIMACY WITH PARTNERS WHO HAVE ASPERGER'S

Aston, M. 2003. *Aspergers in Love: Couple Relationships and Family Affairs.* London: Jessica Kingsley Publishers.

Aston, M. C. 2001. *The Other Half of Asperger Syndrome: A Guide to Living in an Intimate Relationship with a Partner Who Has Asperger Syndrome.* London: The National Autistic Society.

Bentley, K. 2007. *Alone Together: Making an Asperger Marriage Work.* London: Jessica Kingsley Publishers.

Hendrickx, S., and K. Newton. 2007. *Asperger Syndrome: A Love Story.* London: Jessica Kingsley Publishers.

Jacobs, B. 2006. *Loving Mr. Spock: Understanding an Aloof Lover—Could It Be Asperger Syndrome?* New ed. London: Jessica Kingsley Publishers.

Simone, R. 2009. *22 Things a Woman Must Know: If She Loves a Man with Asperger's Syndrome.* London: Jessica Kingsley Publishers.

Slater-Walker, G., and C. Slater-Walker. 2002. *An Asperger Marriage.* London: Jessica Kingsley Publishers.

Stanford, A. 2003. *Asperger Syndrome and Long-Term Relationships.* London: Jessica Kingsley Publishers.

TO HELP YOU DEAL WITH ANGER

Eifert, G. H., M. McKay, and J. P. Forsyth. 2006. *ACT on Life, Not on Anger: The New Acceptance & Commitment Therapy Guide to Problem Anger.* Oakland, CA: New Harbinger Publications.

Lerner, H. 1997. *The Dance of Anger: A Woman's Guide to Changing the Patterns of Intimate Relationships.* New York: HarperCollins Publishers.

BY ADULTS WITH AUTISM OR ASPERGER'S SYNDROME

Carley, M. J. 2008. *Asperger's from the Inside Out: A Supportive and Practical Guide for Anyone with Asperger's Syndrome.* New York: Penguin Group.

Grandin, T. 1996. *Thinking in Pictures: And Other Reports from My Life with Autism.* New York: Vintage Books.

Grandin, T., and S. Barron. 2005. *Unwritten Rules of Social Relationships: Decoding Social Mysteries through the Unique Perspectives of Autism.* Arlington, TX: Future Horizons.

Holliday Willey, L. 1999. *Pretending to Be Normal: Living with Asperger's Syndrome.* London: Jessica Kingsley Publishers.

Newport, J. 2001. *Your Life Is Not a Label: A Guide to Living Fully with Autism and Asperger's Syndrome for Parents, Professionals, and You.* Arlington, TX: Future Horizons.

Newport, J., and M. Newport. 2007. *Mozart and the Whale: An Asperger's Love Story.* With J. Dodd. New York: Touchstone.

Robison, J. E. 2007. *Look Me in the Eye: My Life with Asperger's.* New York: Crown Publishers.

———. 2011. *Be Different: Adventures of a Free-Range Aspergian with Practical Advice for Aspergians, Misfits, Families, and Teachers.* New York: Crown Archetype.

Shore, S. 2003. *Beyond the Wall: Personal Experiences with Autism and Asperger Syndrome.* 2nd ed. Shawnee Mission, KS: Autism Asperger Publishing Company.

Tammet, D. 2007. *Born on a Blue Day: Inside the Extraordinary Mind of an Autistic Savant.* New York: Free Press.

Williams, D. 1994. *Somebody Somewhere: Breaking Free from the World of Autism.* New York: Three Rivers Press.

———. 1999. *Nobody Nowhere: The Remarkable Autobiography of an Autistic Girl.* London: Jessica Kingsley Publishers.

Websites and Organizations

A number of supportive organizations offer information for people with Asperger's syndrome and their partners. You can also find online support groups through many of the sites listed here.

Asperger Syndrome Education Network (ASPEN) includes helpful resources for family and friends of people with Asperger's syndrome on its website: www.aspennj.org.

The Asperger Syndrome and High Functioning Autism Association of New York provides support, information, and useful resources: www.ahany.org.

The Asperger's Association of New England (AANE) has a helpful website with a few resources specifically for partners of adults with AS: www.aane.org.

Aspires (Asperger Syndrome Partners and Individuals: Resources, Encouragement, and Support) devotes a website to issues that partners and family members face: http.aspires-relationships.com.

Autism Research Centre (ARC) in Cambridge, UK, directed by Simon Baron-Cohen, provides his research on its website, including the EQ, the SQ, and other tests developed there, such as the Adult Asperger Assessment (AAA) and the Eyes Test: www.autismresearchcentre.com.

Autism Research Institute offers a website that provides research-based information: www.autism.com.

Autism Society (USA) provides a website dedicated to information regarding autism and the autism spectrum: www.autism-society.org.

Autism Speaks, a national science and advocacy organization, offers a helpful website: www.autismspeaks.org.

Autistics Speak provides a voice for people on the autism spectrum: autisticsspeak.wordpress.com.

The Global and Regional Asperger Syndrome Partnership (GRASP) focuses on helping teens and adults on the autism spectrum by providing information and advocacy: www.grasp.org.

The Interactive Autism Network (IAN) site provides articles and a discussion forum with information from people with autism spectrum conditions, partners, family members, and autism experts: www.iancommunity.org.

The National Autistic Society (UK) offers extensive information and resources on its website, plus this website links to autism resources and societies all over the world: www.autism.org.uk.

OASIS (Online Asperger Syndrome Information and Support @ MAAP) contains articles, links to support groups and professional help, and recommended reading: www.aspergersyndrome.org.

WrongPlanet.net is a web community that provides blogs, discussions, and articles for neurologically diverse people and their loved ones: www.wrongplanet.net.

Contact the Author

I would love to hear your relationship story, including your own successes or failures in loving someone with Asperger's syndrome. You can "like" my practice, Alternative Choices, on Facebook and add your voice to our discussions. You can also check out our website at alternativechoices.com, offered from the independent psychology practice I cofounded in 1992. Our practice offers short- and long-term therapy solutions for a wide range of people and problems. We work with many people of all ages on the autism spectrum, as well as their partners, friends, and families. You can e-mail me confidentially at cariel@alternativechoices.com.

References

American Psychiatric Association (APA). 1994. *Diagnostic and Statistical Manual of Mental Disorders (DSM-IV)*. 4th ed. Washington, DC: American Psychiatric Association.

———. 2000. *Diagnostic and Statistical Manual of Mental Disorders (DSM-IV-TR)*. 4th ed., text rev. Washington, DC: American Psychiatric Association.

Asperger, H. (1944) 1991. "Autistic Psychopathy in Childhood." Translated and annotated by U. Frith. In *Autism and Asperger Syndrome*, 1st ed., edited by U. Frith, 37–92. Cambridge: Cambridge University Press.

———. 1979. "Problems of Infantile Autism." *Communication* 13:45–52.

Aston, M. 2009. *The Asperger Couple's Workbook: Practical Advice and Activities for Couples and Counsellors*. London: Jessica Kingsley Publishers.

Attwood, T. 1998. *Asperger's Syndrome: A Guide for Parents and Professionals*. London: Jessica Kingsley Publishers.

———. 2007a. *The Complete Guide to Asperger's Syndrome*. London: Jessica Kingsley Publishers.

————. 2007b. "Relationship Problems of Adults with Asperger's Syndrome." *Good Autism Practice (GAP)* 8 (1):13–24.

Baron-Cohen, S. 2003. *The Essential Difference: Men, Women, and the Extreme Male Brain.* New York: Basic Books.

Baron-Cohen, S., J. Richler, D. Bisarya, N. Gurunathan, and S. Wheelwright. 2003. "The Systemizing Quotient: An Investigation of Adults with Asperger Syndrome or High-Functioning Autism, and Normal Sex Differences." *Philosophical Transactions of the Royal Society* 358 (1430):361–740. doi:10.1098/rstb.2002.1206.

Baron-Cohen, S., and S. Wheelwright. 2004. "The Empathy Quotient: An Investigation of Adults with Asperger Syndrome or High-Functioning Autism, and Normal Sex Differences." *Journal of Autism and Developmental Disorders* 34 (2):163–75.

Beck, A. T. 1988. *Love Is Never Enough: How Couples Can Overcome Misunderstandings, Resolve Conflicts, and Solve Relationship Problems through Cognitive Therapy.* New York: Harper and Row Publishers.

Boyle, C. A., K. van Naarden Braun, and M. Yeargin-Allsopp. 2005. "Prevalence and Genetic Epidemiology of Developmental Disabilities." In *Genetics of Developmental Disabilities*, edited by M. G. Butler and F. J. Meaney, 693–742. Boca Raton, FL: Taylor and Francis Group.

Centers for Disease Control (CDC). 2011. "What We've Learned about Autism Spectrum Disorder." www.cdc.gov/Features/Counting Autism/ (accessed July 28, 2011).

DiCicco-Bloom, E., C. Lord, L. Zwaigenbaum, E. Courchesne, S. R. Dager, C. Schmitz, R. T. Schultz, J. Crawley, and L. J. Young. 2006. "The Developmental Neurobiology of Autism Spectrum Disorder." *Journal of Neuroscience* 26 (26):6897–6906.

Epstein, R. 2010. "How Science Can Help You Fall (and Stay) in Love." *Scientific American Mind*, January/February. 26–33.

Fein, E., and S. Schneider. 1995. *The Rules: Time-Tested Secrets for Capturing the Heart of Mr. Right.* New York: Warner Books.

Gibran, K. (1923) 1972. *The Prophet*. New York: Alfred A. Knopf. Reprint by same. Citation refers to the later printing.

Goldberg, N. 2010. *Writing Down the Bones: Freeing the Writer Within*. Expanded (hardcover) ed. Boston: Shambhala Publications.

Gottman, J. M., and N. Silver. 1999. *The Seven Principles for Making Marriage Work: A Practical Guide from the Country's Foremost Relationship Expert*. New York: Three Rivers Press.

Helgoe, L. 2010. "Revenge of the Introvert." *Psychology Today* 43 (5):54–61.

Hénault, I. 2006. *Asperger's Syndrome and Sexuality: From Adolescence through Adulthood*. London: Jessica Kingsley Publishers.

Hendrickx, S., and K. Newton. 2007. *Asperger Syndrome: A Love Story*. London: Jessica Kingsley Publishers.

Holliday Willey, L. 1999. *Pretending to Be Normal: Living with Asperger's Syndrome*. London: Jessica Kingsley Publishers.

Kanner, L. 1943. "Autistic Disturbances of Affective Contact." *Nervous Child* 2:217–50.

Kessler, R. C., P. Berglund, O. Demler, R. Jin, K. R. Merikangas, and E. E. Walters. 2005. "Lifetime Prevalence and Age-of-Onset Distributions of DSM-IV Disorders in the National Comorbidity Survey Replication." *Archives of General Psychiatry* 62 (6):593–602.

Mayer, M. 2009. *Adam*. Directed by Max Mayer. Los Angeles: Fox Searchlight Pictures.

National Institutes of Health (NIH). 2009. "Risk of Autism Tied to Genes That Influence Brain Cell Connections." *NIH News*. Bethesda, MD: National Institutes of Health. www.nih.gov/news /health/apr2009/ninds-28.htm (accessed April 19, 2011).

Newschaffer, C. J., L. A. Croen, J. Daniels, E. Giarelli, J. K. Grether, S. E. Levy, D. S. Mandell, L. A. Miller, J. Pinto-Martin, J. Reaven, A. M. Reynolds, C. E. Rice, D. Schendel, and G. C. Windham. 2007. "The Epidemiology of Autism Spectrum Disorders." *Annual Review of Public Health* 28:235–58.

Regier, D. A., D. S. Rae, W. E. Narrow, C. T. Kaelber, and A. F. Schatzberg. 1998. "Prevalence of Anxiety Disorders and Their Comorbidity with Mood and Addictive Disorders." *British Journal of Psychiatry* 173 (Suppl. 34):24–28.

Robison, J. E. 2007. *Look Me in the Eye: My Life with Asperger's.* New York: Crown Publishers.

Shore, S. 2002. "Dating, Marriage, and Autism: A Personal Perspective." *Advocate*, 4th ed., 24–27.

Smith Myles, B., M. L. Trautman, and R. L. Schelvan. 2004. *The Hidden Curriculum: Practical Solutions for Understanding Unstated Rules in Social Situations.* Shawnee Mission, KS: Autism Asperger Publishing Company.

Taylor, F. W. 1911. *The Principles of Scientific Management.* Norwood, MA: The Plimpton Press.

Viorst, J. 2003. *Grown-Up Marriage: What We Know, Wish We Had Known, and Still Need to Know about Being Married.* New York: The Free Press.

Wallerstein, J. S., and S. Blakeslee. 2003. *What About the Kids? Raising Your Children Before, During, and After Divorce.* New York: Hyperion.

Cindy N. Ariel, PhD, is a psychologist in Philadelphia, PA, with over twenty years of experience working with people dealing with Asperger's syndrome. She is coeditor of Voices from the Spectrum.

Foreword writer **Stephen Shore, EdD,** is assistant professor of education at Adelphi University. He has Asperger's syndrome himself and is an internationally known author, consultant, and presenter on issues related to the autism spectrum.